Buried in Denmark

The allied airmen in
Svino Commonwealth War Graves

Mette Magnusson

Buried in Denmark
The allied airmen in
Svino Commonwealth War Graves

- In remembrance of P/O Sydney Nelson Cross, whom I have never met but whose dear family became my New Zealand family

Mette Magnusson

Translated from Danish by the author
Copyright 2017 – Mette Magnusson
Publishing company: Books on Demand GmbH, Copenhagen, Denmark
Production: Books on demand GmbH, Norderstedt, Germany
The book is produced after on-Demand-process

ISBN 9788771883497

During World War II about 300 allied aircrafts crashed over Denmark.
A little less than 100 crew members survived and were rescued to safety in Sweden.
Approximately 300 crew members survived but were subsequently captured by the Germans and sent to a POW camp.
It is estimated that around 500 airmen died in the oceans around Denmark and were never found.
1160 dead allied airmen were buried in Denmark - of which 134 Americans, who later were exhumed and taken out of Denmark - some for reburial in the United States, others to be buried in one of the American cemeteries in the Netherlands, Belgium and Luxembourg.
Eight American airmen are still buried in Denmark.
At Svino cemetery 108 allied airmen were buried during the war.
They were young men with hope and wishes for a future, they never even came to experience. Yet in many ways they became part of that future.
They live on in the hearts of their families and they still touch our hearts, when we visit their graves and read at the tombstones, how young they were.
They paid with their lives for the world they handed on to us.
Let us cherish this world in the hope of a future peaceful life in it - from love to it, and out of respect for those who fought for it.
This little book tells the story of Svino Memorial Grove and some of the destinies attached to this place, and it is written in honor and deep respect - not only of the fallen airmen, who were buried at Svino cemetery during World War II - but also of the families to these young men, who by their death lost a son, a husband, a brother or a father, and for whom this loss has provided them with a sorrow, they will always have to carry with them.

> They shall grow not old, as we that are left grow old:
> Age shall not weary them, nor the years condemn.
> At the going down of the sun and in the morning
> We will remember them.
>
> *- Laurence Binyon (1869-1943)*

In order to publish this little book, I am indebted to several people:

Thanks to Chief of the Air Staff, Major General Max A.L.T. Nielsen for his goodwill towards this book about Svino Memorial Grove and the allied airmen buried there.

Thanks to Brigadier General Steen Harboe Hartov for help and correction of the chapter on Airbase Avno.

And finally many thanks to the former Chief Sergeant Boeggild Gammelgaard, who saw the importance of publishing this book and helped it on the way and made publishing possible.

Mette Magnusson

Contents

Every year on May 4th, we commemorate Denmark's liberation throughout the country. Especially one of these commemorations is close to the Royal Danish Air Force's heart and history, i.e. the Commemoration at the Svino Cemetery, where more than 100 allied airmen from WW2 found their final resting place.

With her work on the Svino Commonwealth War Graves vicar Mette Magnusson succeeded in assemble an important part of history, we must never forget. With her tenacious work on Svino Memorial Grove the danger of oblivion of this specific chapter of our common history is over.

Relatives and descendants of the young airmen who paid the ultimate price for our shared values of freedom and peace in the world, now has a deserved and readable memoir about their loved one's final resting place. History buffs have been provided with yet another read worthy story and a comprehensive document that can complement and inspire further historical work.

All readers of Mette Magnusson's book will gain a deeper understanding of the many different sides of society that stand behind the establishment of Svino Memorial Grove, including the huge effort granted by volunteers, individual citizens and associations. Their work has been instrumental and a prerequisite for our possibility as a nation to honour, those who honour is due, and internationally demonstrate that Denmark does not take any sacrifices of our allies for granted. The Royal Danish Air Force is proud to contribute to the commemoration and honour our fallen colleagues with a "Missing Man" formation of aircraft from the Royal Danish Flying School.

As Chief of the Air Staff, I welcome this book, not just as interesting and enlightening reading, but also as a serious reminder about the fact that today, we are still dependent on skilled, brave men and women ready to provide a selfless effort for our common values and all that is worth fighting for.

Enjoy your reading!

Karup
17/04/2017

M.A.L.T. NIELSEN
Major General
Chief of the Air Staff

The area
– Svino

The area of Svino, where 108 allied airmen were buried during World War II, is a peninsula in the southwestern part of Zealand between Naestved and Vordingborg and about 90 km southwest of Copenhagen.

It is in many ways a rural and remote area, and this was the reason why the Germans chose Svino as one of the five central cemeteries for dead allied airmen. (The other four central cemeteries, appointed by the Germans, are found in Aabenraa, Esbjerg, Lemvig and Frederikshavn.)

Svino is - besides being rural and remote - also a beautiful little corner of Denmark marked by ancient traditions.

For example there is a guild of farmers at Svino, which has existed for several hundred years, although it now mostly serves as a social club, giving a party every year at Michael's day, September 29.

There are two explanations for this somewhat curious name "Svino" (the Danish word "svin" means pig).

One is that there in the sea off Svino were many porpoises, and therefore the good porpoise catch has given name to the place – porpoise is in Danish "marsvin".

Another explanation is that there should have been unusually many pigs on Svino.

A fact is, however, that there is now a relatively large seal population around Svinø and Avno, and therefore you might easily imagine that the first explanation was the real one.

Svino harbor, where the porpoises previously were landed, is situated at a narrow stream between Dybso and Svino.

In the middle of the 1800s, many of the goods to be traded in Kong, which, incidentally, at this time was a thriving commercial village, were sailed to and from Svino harbor. Now, the port is only in use for quite a few sport sailors and fishermen, and it's where "The Dybso-man" can travel to and from his home on Dybso, the tiny island just northwest of Svino.

The entire coastal area along Svino beach and the small harbor is a nice area, both for people who love to fish, and for those who just like to go for a walk in the lovely countryside.

Until about 1600 Svino was a real island - and not as today a peninsula - and in the Middle Ages Svino belonged to Roskilde bishopric, but in 1410 the bishop gave away Svino to Gavno, which at that time was a nunnery.

Sometime after the Reformation (1536), the island was given free but preserved some attachment to Gavno, and in the late 1600s the barony of Gavno actually owned Svino. The farmers from Svino therefore for a number of years had to work at the estate of Gavno. They had to bring both horses and carriages for the work, and the trip to Gavno therefore went overland past Kostraede and around the inlet of Dybso. Now and then Svino peasants on their way to Gavno began fighting with fellows from other places, and they therefore had a reputation of having a bad temper.

Besides regular farming there was also dealt a lot with both horses and cattle from Svino.

Residents of Svino loved to party, and none of life's celebrations were allowed to go unnoticed. And so it still is.

In the 1940s, when the allied airmen were buried at Svino, the small community was still marked by farming. There were also a couple of small grocery stores, and then there was a school.
Furthermore, there was a church, and it was recent. As a matter of fact, it was at that time only about 40 years old.

The Church

- Svino Church

Svino church seen from southwest.

If you are standing just outside Svino Church, you can see very far.
To the southeast you will see the inlet of Avno and Knudshoved spit, and to the northwest you can see the inlet of Dybso.
South of the church you will find Svino cemetery, and north of the church you find Svino Memorial Grove with the graves of the allied airmen.
Svino became an independent parish in October 2010. Until then, the current Svino parish was a church district in Kong parish, and Kong Church can actually just be seen to the northeast. Therefore, all the allied airmen are buried at Svino but in Kong parish, as it was then called.
Svino parish now has joint parish council with Kong parish and belongs to Stege-Vordingborg deanery under Roskilde diocese.
 The church was built in 1900 on the initiative of the women from Svino.
It is said that after they have been for worship on Sundays in Kong Church, the women had difficulty in getting the men back home from the subsequent and compulsory visit to Kong Inn. The women became tired of waiting for the men and therefore they started rising money for their own church on Svino.
They were well supported by the then parish vicar Jacob Holdt, who also would rather like a real church on Svino, instead of having to celebrate services in Svino school room from time to time.
The men from Svino gradually became accustomed with the idea of having their own church and set up a church committee.

Architect Hans Glahn, Nykobing F. designed the church and master builder Lars Hansen, Praestoe built it.

12.600kr. was allocated at the Finance Act in 1899, and among the locals additional 10.000 Danish Kroner were collected. It became approx. 22.000kr, and that was exactly what it at that time cost to build the church.

Much in and around the church are gifts - including the plot on which the church is built.

The estate of Gavno donated the altarpiece, which is a replica of the altarpiece in Rosenholm Chapel in Jutland. It was painted by A. Dorph. It is painted on wood, depicting the crucified Jesus. In front of the cross a person, who presumably must be the disciple John, is kneeling.

Also the baptismal dish is a gift from the estate of Gavno, while the baptismal font is processed by Stonemason Hans Jacob Hansen from a large stone, he found in a field near Allerslev near Praestoe.

The church bell of iron was made in the Netherlands.

The chalice and the disc comes from a warship as part of the altar service which since the bombardment of Copenhagen in 1807 had been in the custody of the then Ministry of Culture, and from 1894 these altar services were given away to new churches. Here Svino Church was considered.

From a local farm, Munkehojgaard, small cups for use in the communion of the church, were donated.

On the altar there are four candlesticks, two three-armed and two for the big ritual candles. The two three-armed silver candlesticks were donated by people at the local large farm, Ostergaard.

Of the two church chandeliers one is donated by the women from Svino, the second by a farmer, Peder Nielsen, Vestervang Farm.

The large crocheted Lord's Prayer in the church is done by Hildeborg Hansen from Dybso-road. She was a telephone operator at what was then called the West Svino telephone exchange.

Many things in the church as well as the entire history of the church witness of a strong local desire for a church on Svino.

In the early 1990s a real organ was set up in the church. Until then and since the church was build, music was performed on a harmonium.

Likewise, the church in the late 1990s received a nave, a copy of "The Norwegian Lion", built by Finn Knudsen, Ballerup, who after a visit to Svino church had noticed that there wasn't any nave in the church, and he therefore would like to build and donate one.

Over the exit door from the church to the porch a small statuette was put up in 2015. It is a gift from a daughter, Rosalind Elliott, to one of the buried airmen Wilfred John Parsons. The figurine is a mini replica of a large monument in rough sheet iron, which is displayed at the airfield Lisset near the English town of Bridlington. This airfield was home to RAF no.158 Squadron. (More about this on p. 80)

In the small porch is a staircase to the tower. In the porch is also the pastor board along with some gifts from visitors.

Outside the church you can sit on the bench and enjoy the scenery of Zealand and the view towards the inlet of Dybso, or you can pay a visit to the Memorial Grove for the allied airmen.

The Airbase

- Avno airbase

When I came to Kong and Svino as a vicar in 1989, it was so nice to hear the small training aircrafts from Avno airbase come buzzing over the vicarage in Kong, and I was told by the then head of the airbase and flying school at Avno, Lieutenant Colonel Donald Thestrup, that the students actually often were given the task of navigating towards Kong Church tower.
It ended abruptly; however, when the airbase on February 1, 1993 were shut down and dismantled both as an air base and as a flying school and the flying school was removed to Karup.
A period which began 63 years earlier was suddenly over.

In 1930 the Ministry of the Navy leased 40 hectares of land from proprietary Preisz on the big farm Avnogaarden.
A hangar and a wooden building was build which came to house classrooms and workshops. In addition, three barracks were built to give room for officers, flight engineers, servicemen and a cook.
The Danish Air Force did not exist at this time, so it was the Navy that would train student pilots in this so called Naval Air Station.
In the spring of 1931 the whole lot in all its glory began being used. "Glory" was perhaps not the right word as the primary water was a problem. It was salt water coming out of the taps, and you had at the beginning to fetch drinking water from the farm Avnogaarden. You also in the first years simply had to shut it all down in the winter (or "unrig" as it was called – as it was in the Navy!).
In 1936 The Marine Ministry, however, bought 66 ha land from the farm Avnogaarden, and they built a real barracks and one more hangar. Also, a minor hangar was moved from Ringsted to Avno.
On the whole the year 1936-37 was marked by construction at the Flying School and the Naval Air Station Avno, now belonging to the Navy Air Corps. They built gymnasium and established water drilling that could supply the airfield with good drinking water. There were established facilities in order to be able to accommodate 30 officers and 40 privates and also to train 40 privates.
However, there was no great enthusiasm of having neither to be trained nor to work at Naval Air Station Avno as the place now were called.
Most people thought it was too far away from everything, and therefore they had to try to make conditions inviting. Both the accommodation, but also living and recreational environment had to be attractive. Therefore a piece of forest was acquired from Avnogaarden.

The beautiful barracks of Air Field Avno built in 1936-37

The flying school was no more than just well underway when the Second World War broke out.

As Denmark on April 9th, 1940 was occupied by the Germans, they however, had initially forgotten Naval Air Station Avno, but two days later a message came from Copenhagen that the school had to be closed down, and on August 5th, 1940 Avno Naval Air Station was handed over to the Germans.

The Germans established a flying school at Avno that would give pilot candidates for the Luftwaffe basic flying training.

First it was Fliegerausbildungsregiment 22, which was established in Avno but this regiment was soon subject to Fliegerausbildungsregiment 42 which the first two years of the war was established in Neustadt-Glewe, and Avno was then used as a training airfield.

The Germans improved the Naval Air Station Avno with an accommodation hut, two hangars and two huts, some sheds and a control tower, which functioned until 1953, when instead a small glass cabin was put on top of one of the hangars. In 1990 a new control tower was built - unfortunately only three years before the whole airbase was closed down in 1993.

The flying school at Avno was used by the Germans throughout the war.

During the German occupation of Denmark the Germans had 21 accidents on the flying school at Avno, which resulted in six dead persons and five seriously injured. From the Danish side there was throughout the time of the flying school 14 accidents, in which five persons were killed.

When The Flying School after the war again came on Danish hands, they had to manage with only two small training aircraft for the first year, but during the last half year of 1946 15 KZ II T training flights were delivered to Avno.

Another challenge to the airfield was that during the war a German refugee camp had been established at the airfield, where about 1,000 German refugees lived.

But the refugee camp was soon closed and the refugees were sent to other camps.

In 1950 on October 1th, the Danish Air Force was established and Avno's time as Naval Air Station was over. Instead it became Airbase Avno.

N.M. Schaiffel-Nielsen tells in his book on Airbase Avno that the Danish Air Force initially had a little trouble getting properly organized, but had help from England from Air Vice Marshal Hugh Saunders, RAF, who managed to establish a Flight Tactical command, an Air Material Command and a Training command.

Maintenance of the aircrafts was given a higher priority than actually anything else, but also accommodation conditions were, however, eventually improved significantly.

Throughout the 1950's conditions for the flying students were cramped, and although there were many of them, it was not until 1980 that a new accommodation building could be taken in use.

In addition, Airbase Avnoe and The Flying School were organized with a chef, an operation section, an administration section, a stock section and an airbase squadron who was given the number: 563.

It were officers in the Navy or the Army, which initially could apply for admission to The Flying School, but later the requirements were changed so that you did not necessarily have to come from either the Navy or Army, but the requirement for admission to The Flying School was simply that you had a solid education along with a good physique and a stable psyche.

From 1971 also women were admitted as student pilots at The Flying School, and they were met with the same requirements as the male students.

The relationship between flight instructors and students also changed. As in all other educational institutions also the flying instructors became more and more supervisors, and a friendlier tone developed instead of the more old-fashioned commanding tone that was prevalent in The Flying School's early days.

The requirements to the students however, were not relaxed. There were high demands and therefore also a high dropout rate during the training. Only the best came through the needle eye.

The flight student's newer and more modern accommodation

In the latter half of the 1980s ideas were put forward of a national pilot training, which could also benefit civilian companies. There was granted funds for and built a new control tower at Avno, but some agreements went by the board, which resulted in the opposite of a development of Airbase Avno - namely, a winding up.

In the late 1992 they began to close down, and on February 1th, 1993 the flag was hauled down and the key turned on.

Airbase Avno was now past.

An so was the pleasant buzz from the small trainer planes navigating towards the church tower in Kong.

But the buildings remained.

The impressive headquarters was in a period used by the National Police as a course site, but that also came to an end in 2010.

A few years later the Red Cross came along and established asylum center.

This is also closed down now, and currently (2016) the buildings are empty.

Control Tower and operations sections have been converted into a Nature center, and shelters and trails have been established in the beautiful countryside that surrounds the former airbase, and the place is well worth a visit - only it's a little sad to pass by the empty barracks on the way out there!

Hangar, control tower and operation section, now converted to Avno Naturecenter

The War

- World War II in Danish airspace

Early in the war the RAF began to lay out mines in the Danish waters. But also other activities caused that the RAF aircrafts often found themselves in Danish airspace. They attacked various targets in Denmark, occupied by the Germans, and they threw down weapons to the Danish resistance movement, especially in the last years of the war, when the resistance movement was well organized.

Furthermore, Denmark was on the route, when the Allies flew from England to Germany and Poland on bombing raids.

A number of flights were also the SOE flights (Special Operations Executives flights whose missions were to "drop" weapons or manpower for espionage or sabotage).

It was extremely dangerous for the airmen to fly through Danish airspace. Most of the downed allied aircrafts crashed, because they were hit by German anti-aircraft missiles - also called Flak after the German word 'Flugabwehrkanone' - or they had perhaps been in direct confrontation with a German fighter.

The crashes intensified in step with the allied overflying intensified, as the war progressed, and since not all crashes were observed and recorded, it is very likely that the number of downed allied aircrafts is significantly higher than the approximately 250 registered crashes. It is assumed that there were indeed about 300 allied aircrafts, which crashed over Danish territory during the war. The crew of the aircrafts considered (there were usually seven and rare times eight crew members per aircraft) meant that about 2100 to 2200 crew members from the allied countries crashed over Danish territory.

Most of the downed crew died and 1160 airmen from the Royal Air Force (RAF), Royal Canadian Air Force (RCAF), Royal Australian Air Force (RAAF), Royal New Zealand Air Force (RNAF) and the United States of American Air Force (USAAF) were buried in Denmark. Of these, 134 American airmen were later exhumed and taken out of Denmark.

Moreover, there were up to 500 crew members, who were never found, and presumably had disappeared in the sea.

In 1980 in Tuborg Harbour in Copenhagen a memorial stone was erected to honor the airmen who disappeared in the seas around Denmark. The memorial was unveiled by H. M. Queen Ingrid on May 5th, 1980.

Finally, approx. 400 airmen survived the crashes, but most of them were subsequently captured by the Germans. About 90 airmen escaped in one way or another out of Denmark to the neutral Sweden.

The first surviving RAF, who succeeded going to Sweden, was Donald Smith (in April 1943). However, he died in 1998 and his urn was interned at Svino cemetery in 1999(see more on p.59)

Most plane crashes took place in Jutland and only about a quarter of all crashes occurred in the rest of the country and in the seas around Denmark.

At Svino cemetery 108 allied crew members were buried. They came from 32 different crashed planes. A total of 54 airmen were identified crew members from 19 crashed RAF aircrafts, including 3 crashed RNZAF aircrafts, one crashed RCAF aircraft and one crashed RAAF aircraft.

Furthermore, 42 identified Americans from 13 crashed USAAF aircrafts were buried at Svino cemetery.

Furthermore eight unidentified British airmen and four unidentified American airmen were buried at Svino cemetery (two of the four unknown Americans are subsequently identified).

In many aircrafts (not the US) the crew was mixed from different countries.

At Svino cemetery are thus buried eight airmen from the Royal New Zealand Air Force, eight from the Royal Canadian Air Force, four from the Royal Australian Air Force and 42 from the Royal Air Force - including 2 from the then Rhodesia - now Zimbabwe - as well as one airman from Ireland.

Furthermore, 46 Americans were buried, but they were later exhumed.

From the 32 aircrafts whose crew members were buried at Svino, the 25 were bombers and the 7 were mine layers.

The 32 aircrafts came from 24 different squadrons.

3 aircrafts from RAF SQD. 9 (bomber) (motto: Per Noctem volamus (We fly through the night))
Crashed 16.5 1942, 23.9 1942, 24.9 1942

3 aircrafts from RAF SQD. 77 (bomber) (Motto: Esse quam potius videri (To be rather than to seem)) Crashed 30.3 1943, 24.4 1944, 15.2 1945

3 aircrafts from RNZAF SQD.75 (minelayer) (motto: Ake Ake Kia Kaha (Maori) (Always, always: Be strong)) Crashed 28.4 1943, 29.4 1943, 12.9 1944

1 aircraft from RAF SQD. 50 (bomber) (motto: Sic fidem servamus (Thus we maintain faith))
Crashed 9.5 1942

1 aircraft from RAF SQD.10 (bomber) (motto: Rem acu tangent (To hit the target))
Crashed 1.10 1942

1 aircraft from RAF SQD.7 (bomber) (motto: Per diem, per noctem (During day, during night)) Crashed 21.4 1943

1 aircraft from RAF SQD.158 (bomber) (motto: Strength in unity)
Crashed 21.4 1943

1 aircraft from RAF SQD.90 (bomber) (motto: Celer (Quick))
Crashed 21.4 1943

1 aircraft from RAAF SQD.460 (bomber) (motto: Strike and return)
Crashed 4.9 1943

1 aircraft from RAF SQD.619 (bomber) (motto: Ad altoria (Towards higher things))
Crashed 16.2 1944

1 aircraft from RAF SQD.102 (minelayer) (motto: Tentate a perficite (Try it and complete it))
Crashed 24.4 1944

1 aircraft from RCAF SQD.405 (bomber) (motto: Ducimus (We lead))
Crashed 17.8 1944

1 aircraft from RAF SQD.44 (bomber) (motto: Fulmina regis iusta (The king's lightning is righteous)).
Crashed 7.3 1945. This squadron was originally based in Essex but was renamed in 1941 (no. 44 Rhodesia) in respect of Rhodesia's contribution to British warfare. (25% of land + air staff was from Rhodesia)

3 aircrafts from the USAAF SQD. 728 (bomber)
Crashed 20.2 in 1944 and two flights 9/4 1944

1 aircraft from USAAF SQD.334 (bomber)
Crashed 13.6 1943

1 aircraft from USAAF SQD.336 (bomber)
Crashed 13.6 1943

1 aircraft from USAAF SQD.335 (bomber)
Crashed 13.6 1943

1 aircraft from USAAF SQD.322 (bomber)
Crashed 9.10 1943

1 aircraft from USAAF SQD.755 (bomber)
Crashed 9.4 1944

1 aircraft from USAAF SQD.339 (bomber)
Crashed 9.4 1944

1 aircraft from the USAF SQD.786 (bomber)
Crashed 9.4 1944

1 aircraft from USAAF SQD.563 (bomber)
Crashed 9.4 1944

1 aircraft from USAAF SQD.427 (bomber)
Crashed 29.4 1944

1 aircraft from USAAF SQD.366 (bomber)
Crashed 4.8 1944

The cemeteries

As mentioned above, 1160 allied airmen were buried in Denmark during the war.
They were buried at no less than 119 different cemeteries.
After the American airmen in 1948-49 were exhumed and taken out of Denmark,
allied airmen are still buried at 108 different Danish cemeteries.
At some of the cemeteries only one or maybe a few airmen are buried. At other
cemeteries many airmen are buried. This is because the airmen in the beginning of
the war usually were taken to the nearest cemetery and buried there. But after a few
years of war, the Germans chose to establish central cemeteries, where the fallen
allied airmen could be buried.

Denmark was then divided into five zones, each of them with a central cemetery. In that way it was supposed to be convenient to administer and manage the funerals of the allied airmen.

Aabenraa was made central cemetery for fallen airmen over southern Jutland (144 British and 7 Polish airmen and 4 (now exhumed) Americans).

Esbjerg became the central cemetery of the south west and mid Jutland (271 British, 1 Polish and 26 (now exhumed) Americans).

Lemvig was made central cemetery for the mid-western Jutland (42 British, 1 Polish and 7 (now exhumed) Americans).

Frederikshavn became central cemetery of the northern Jutland area (61 British, 1 Polish and 4 (now exhumed) Americans).

Finally Svino was made central cemetery for downed allied airmen over the southern and western Zealand, Lolland, Falster and Moen (62 British and 46 (now exhumed) Americans).

Fyn and the northern part of Zealand did not belong to any of the five zones, but both Assens (19 British and 9 (now exhumed) Americans) and Odense (22 British and 3 (now exhumed) Americans) have quite a lot allied graves.

In addition, 24 allied airmen were buried in Copenhagen at Bispebjerg Cemetery.

However the division of Denmark into those five zones doesn't seem to have been entirely consistent, as actually throughout the war some airmen actually were buried in the same way as in the beginning of the war - that is at the nearest cemetery to the actual crash site or to the spot, where the dead airman was found.

The German choice of central cemeteries could - when it came to Aabenraa, Esbjerg, Lemvig and Frederikshavn - be explained in that way that it was reasonably large and central cities - and also cemeteries - in each of their zone - but why on earth was Svino chosen as a central cemetery?

- Well, it is reported that it was the German commander from the occupied airbase Avno who should have proposed it, but as a matter of fact no document or the like in the archive of Svino memorial grove can confirm that the Germans actually did choose Svino as central cemetery, but that was nevertheless how it turned out.

Svino became one of Denmark's five central cemeteries for allied airmen from World War II, and further more Svino became the cemetery where most American airmen were buried.

In a report to the bishop from February 28, 1945 on religious matters in Kong parish with Svino Church District, of which a copy is to be found in the "Liber Daticus"(see p.116) of the parish, the Reverend Johannes Lindelov (vicar of Kong and Svino 1925-1952) writes:

"A special circumstance here in the parish is that until September 17, 1944 about 100 crashed allied airmen from southern part of Zealand etc. have been buried at Svino on behalf of the Wehrmacht at Avno. Until Easter 1943 by a German vicar - since by me until Easter 1944. Since then without any clergyman. BUT with graveside ceremony in the presence of the congregation at Sunday services after each interment.
Since September 17, 1944 no funerals. The corpses are probably dug down into the beach, where they are found, but as a matter of fact we have a "warrior cemetery" with 100 graves. "

Some 5 years later, the Rev. Lindelov in connection with the opening of Svino Memorial Grove as a Commonwealth War Graves cemetery has written and stated more precisely in "Liber Daticus":

"Svino memorial grove for allied airmen shot down over southern Denmark during the Second World War from 1940 to 1945 and buried by Reverend Lindelov in a number of 108: 62 British and 46 American airmen - inaugurated on May 5th 1950 with the participation of representatives of the Ministry of Ecclesiastical Affairs, the British Embassy, the prefect of Praestoe County, Roskilde Bishop, etc. "

At that time, the Americans, however had been exhumed and taken out of the country.
Remaining were the 62 British airmen.

The burials at Svino

The first burial of an allied airman at Svino cemetery took place on May 13, 1942 and was conducted by the German Wehrmacht. In fact, it was a German army chaplain from Copenhagen, who traveled to Svino and conducted the funeral.
It was - although the Germans buried an enemy - a great military funeral with the firing of a salute of honor and attended by several German military personnel in addition to the German chaplain who conducted the funeral. Also the chief of police from Vordingborg attended.
Soon after more funerals took place - also conducted by the German chaplain.
These funerals of course were to be registered in the parish register, and therefore Reverend Lindelov had to be informed about them, although he himself was not in charge of the funerals, so that he could establish the correct personal information about the deceased in the church register.
However it seemed to be rather difficult to get the correct information from the Germans.
There is in the archive of Svino Memorial Grove a small slip of paper concerning funeral number two, a note to the vicar from the Germans, which shortly reads:

"Personalien des Engländers:
Sergeant Gruchy, gefallen am 16. Mai 1942 bei Langö auf Lolland (Dänemark) "
Signed by the Oberarzt u. Truppenarzt from Airbase Avno.

Truppenarzt ...
Dr. Lundby Øt.   Aun?, den 20. Mai 1942

              Herrn
              Lindelov, Johannes
              Kørg pr. Lundby St.

              Personalien des Engländers:

              Sergant G r u c h y , gefallen am 16. Mai 1942
                     bei Langø auf Lolland (Dänemark).

                                          Oberarzt u. Truppenarzt.

But such a note was not enough and certainly not an official documentation for registration in the church register. A few months later the Reverend Lindelov therefore requested from the chief constable of Vordingborg the information which the police might have on the allied airmen, buried by the Germans, and late in the year the vicar received a report on the buried airmen.

The chief constable in Vordingborg attended all funerals of the allied airmen until September 1944, when the Danish police was disbanded. Therefore, it was indeed to the police, Reverend Lindelov should go and ask for information.

In the end of the year 1942, 10 crashed allied airmen have been buried at Svino cemetery and the headline of the information that The Reverend Lindelov received from the Chief of Police in Vordingborg, reads (in German):

"Personalien der 10 beigesetzten englischen Fliegerleichen bez.w. Leichenteile in Svinø".

When it said "body parts", it meant, of course, that it could be difficult to determine the deceased's identity, and often human remains from different dead persons were buried together, which is the case according to this document regarding grave number 3.

There are similar reports like this one from 1942 both from 1943 and 1944 until September 17, 1944, after which the bodies, as Reverend Lindelov wrote (see p. 19), probably was buried where they were found - often in the seashore somewhere along the Danish coast.

From September 1944 the allied airmen were no longer buried at cemeteries, probably due to the war developments. It was in the summer of 1944 that the allied invasion of France took place.

Reverend Lindelov writes in "Liber Daticus" that funeral until Easter 1943 was carried out by the German Wehrmacht, and then onward to Easter 1944, the funerals were carried out by him as the local vicar.

One might imagine that it was too time-consuming and inconvenient for the German chaplain to travel from Copenhagen, where he was and to Svinø to bury the dead airmen.

In an announcement of January 15, 1944 from "The Reichsbevollmächtigte in Dänemark" it says:

"Die Mitwirkung eines Geistlichen ist selbstverständlich gestattet. Soweit ein Wehrmachtgeistlicher nicht zur Verfügung steht, kann ein dänischer Zivilgeistlicher herangezogen werden".

A specific permission was by this announcement given to the Danish vicars to conduct the funerals of the allied airmen, as long as the vicar stuck to the purely ecclesiastical:

„Die Geistlichen haben sich jedoch bei ihrer Tätigkeit auf die kirchlichen Zeremonien zu beschränken und selbstverständlich jede offene oder versteckte Demonstration bei ihren Amtshandlungen zu unterlassen."

However, the church bells could no longer ring at funerals:

"Im Interesse der Aufrechthaltung von Sicherheit und Ordnung bei den derzeitigen Verhältnissen in Dänemark wird das Läuten von Glocken in diesen Fällen nicht gestattet..."

However, in the late 1943 the Germans began to dig down the dead airmen at Svinø cemetery without giving the vicar opportunity to conduct the funerals. This practice continued until September 1944, after which they were no longer buried at the cemetery.

Reverend Lindelov nevertheless found a way out of this too, so that the allied airmen could continue to have a Christian funeral. On Sundays after the service he together with the congregation simply went out to the new graves, where he officiated the graveside ceremony.

He writes about this immediately after the war in a report to Roskilde Diocese:

"During the funerals at Svino episodes sometimes happened; the different German commanders were not all friendly, and at last the vicar was prohibited to conduct the funerals, which then took place as "cattle burials", and when I together with the congregation began to officiate the graveside ceremony the following Sunday: psalm, prayer, a Scripture, prayer, officiate at the gravesite, blessing and hymn - I was told that it was a demonstration and therefore prohibited; sometimes a Bomber circled over our heads during prayers; but I answered: It is no demonstration, and I do not bend for a local command; and then it went very well; nothing happened to us. "

From September 1944, the killed airmen were buried by the Germans, wherever they were found.

After the end of the war - for that reason –five more airmen were buried at Svino.

Two of these airmen were found pretty quickly after the war.

One of them was the 24 years old Flying Officer James Ritchie found at the Vesterhave Beach, the parish of Karrebaek (northwest of Naestved) on May 7 and buried at Svino on May 11, 1945.
The other was Sergeant Ronald Edward Russell, who was found near Knudshoved Spit, north of Vordingborg on June 10 and buried at Svino on June 14, 1945.
It seems as if both were given an honorable and fine funeral.
In the archive of Svino Memorial Grove there is a photo taken at James Ritchie's funeral, and from Russell's funeral, you can find several programs with hymns.

On the back of this photo it says: Capt. Ritchie´s funeral   *James Ritchie*

On the back of the portrait of James Ritchie is written in Pastor Lindelov's handwriting:
"R.A.F. Officer James Ritchie. Born in Scotland October 15, 1920. Died in fire fight over the Great Belt on February 15, 1945. Buried at Svino Memorial Grove on May 11, 1945. "

The program from Russell's funeral shows that it has been a great funeral, during which several hymns have been sung:
"God does all things right"
"Nearer, my God, to you" (in the song sheet in both Danish and English version)
"The great Master comes."
At the grave was sung both a verse from the hymn "Church bell ...." And "Always cheerful when you go."

The third allied airmen buried after the war, was the pilot Alexander Henry Hall. Well, actually Hall was buried during the war already on October 4, 1944 - but by the Germans at Airbase Avno.

In the church register Lindelov has written that Hall was "buried in the seashore" and that he was found by the British on February 6, 1946.

And that is probably wright. Nevertheless, I cannot help wondering that in N.M. Schaiffel-Nielsen's book about Airbase Avno, you can find a photo of Hall's grave. Here it looks rather pretty. It is fenced and equipped with a white cross. The photo was according to Schaiffel-Nielsen taken in 1946, and it must in that case have been in the very beginning of the year, as Hall according to the church register was reburied at Svino on February 10. But perhaps they managed to make the grave tidy immediately after the war, for as Lindelov describes it, you wouldn't imagine a real grave.

I also wonder a bit why Hall had to stay buried at Airbase Avno for more than six months after the war had ended.

In the church register it only says in the annotation box that he is reburied in Svino on the request of the British authorities in Denmark.

The fourth airman, buried after the end of the war, is Sergeant William Christopher Thornton, who perished on March 7, 1945 and was found in Storstrommen (south of Zealand) by a fisherman in June 1946. He was buried on June 23, 1946 as an unknown Canadian airman (although he actually was not from Canada but from

Ireland) at a fine funeral. Here too, song sheets were used at the funeral, a copy of which can be found in the archive of Svino Memorial Grove.

At this funeral was sung the following hymns: "To say goodbye to the world", "Nearer, my God, to You" (in Danish and English).

At the grave: a verse from the "Church bell, not for capitals" and the last verse of "The blessed day."

However, it is rather mysteriously why it was imagined that this airman was a Canadian. It could be because more than a year had passed before he was found, and it therefore probably was difficult to identify who he was and from where he came.

In the church register it is written later about him with a pencil: British Sergeant (More from RAF), and his name is introduced with a completely different handwriting to that of Reverend Lindelov's and therefore probably much later. He is one of the airmen, who have subsequently been identified by the Missing Research enquiry Service.

Thornton is, moreover, erroneously in several places noted as buried in 1945. The correct year, however, is 1946, supported by both church register, burial Protocol and the date on the song sheet.

The last allied airman, who was buried at Svino cemetery, is however the biggest mystery.

He appears neither in the Parish Register nor the Burial Protocol, but nevertheless there is a headstone on the cemetery, stating that he is Australian.

I had not been particularly aware of the fact, that there was an allied airman buried, who actually did not appear anywhere in the church protocols, but during the last half of the 1990s, I had some correspondence with the late chamberlain Colonel Helge Gram, who has done a tremendous work in trying to identify the unidentified allied airmen buried in Denmark during the war.

A portion of the correspondence was about this particular airman, which Helge Gram diligently made me look for information about. But without luck.

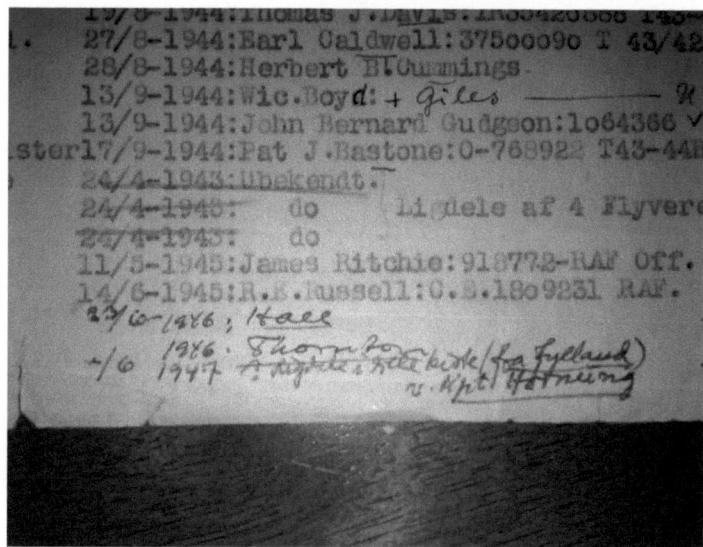

This small note about the burial of the unknown Australian is to be found on a list of buried airmen, where Pastor Lindelov in a corner at the bottom of the paper has written:

"+/6 1947 Body parts in a small coffin from Jutland by Captain Hornung."

Besides there is a similar note, where Lindelov is writing allmost the same and sum up:

"last English airman buried (grave no. 97)June 13, 1947."

I haven't found any other documents about this Australian airman.

The story of the aforementioned small coffin with body parts from Jutland is this: In 1943 on the night between September 3 and 4, an allied aircraft from Squadron 460 - a Lancaster EE138 - who was heading home after a bombing raid over Berlin, crashed.

26

The aircraft was attacked by a German night fighter and crashed near Stadil close to Esbjerg, and eyewitnesses saw the plane explode.

The crew consisted of five British airmen and three Australians and with the aircraft they too exploded into atoms.

However, a body (torso) was found and buried on the spot by the Germans.

The plane had crashed into a wetland from where it was difficult to salvage anything, but a few wallets with names and a name tag was found.

In 1947, in the beginning of June, an attempt was made to drain the wetland and salvage parts from the aircraft, and they also found the torso, buried by the Germans. As at the same time identification exhumation of buried unidentified airmen was going on at Svino, it might have been the reason, why the British authorities decided that the torso from practical reasons could be buried at Svino - even though this airman had not crashed in the area which Svino covered as a central cemetery.

It might of course also be of totally different reasons that the torso came to Svino, for in fact it was the Americans who were doing the exhumations of buried unidentified airmen at Svino in these June days, and it was the British who took care of the torso from Stadil.

However, the torso could not be identified more closely, than they from some material of an Australian battle uniform found on the torso, assumed that the torso belonged to one of the four crew members from the Royal Australian Air Force, who had been on board the aircraft.

Therefore it can be assumed that this torso was either the 30-year-old Cyril Augustine Walsh from the state of Victoria in Australia, or Ewin Garth Carthew, 21 years old, from South Australia or Sydney Milton Forrester, 22 years old and also from South Australia or perhaps Carl Richard Kelaher who was 30 years old and - although he was British and came from London - flew as Squadron Leader in the Royal Australian Air Force.

This information does not exist in any way in the archive of Svino Memorial Grove nor in the church register or in the burial protocol but can be found only on an Australian website for this aircraft. (http://users.tpg.com.au/divinew/Story.html) On this website you can see two documents concerning this aircraft.

One of them is a document from the Royal Australian Air Force's office in London to their office in Melbourne, Australia. The document describes the crash and mention that there were three Australian crew members onboard this aircraft.

The other document shown on the website is a letter from the Royal Air Force dated October 31, 1947, which announces that they on June 3rd 1947 tried to drain the area, where the aircraft crashed at Stadil and rescue parts of the aircraft. It was very difficult (impossible) but they had found a burned body, and some material from an Australian battle uniform. This had been sent to Svino and been buried there on June 13, 1947 in grave no. 97 (a grave number which neither exists in the church register nor in the burial protocol, but had only come into existence as both the British and the Americans by the exhumation and attempt of identification had found and separated body parts from different persons and reburied them consecutively after the last recorded burial no. 93).

Although you can read on the headstone at Svino Memorial Grove that it is an unknown Australian airman who is buried in this place, you can be sure that it is one of the three Australians from this plane - or perhaps the English Squadron Leader, who flew the RAAF.

You just do not know which of them it is.

However, since only this torso is buried at Svino, while the remaining seven crew members from the aircraft still are at the crash site in Stadil, a memorial stone for the whole crew has been erected there. In addition, the previously mentioned Colonel Helge Gram unsuccessfully tried to have the crash site made an official war grave, as you with certainty know that in the ground on this spot are the bodies of seven airmen.

There are no photos or song sheets from the funeral of this Australian airman. And furthermore he is not to be found in either parish or burial protocol, and it does surprise me a bit. Did he have a proper funeral, or has he just been buried?

I have not been able to find answers to that, but it seems a little odd if it should be the case, when the other four dead airmen, who were buried immediately after the war, have had so fine funerals.

Perhaps the explanation may be found in the fact that exhumation and identification was going on at the cemetery of Svino in these June days 1947, and locals were therefore denied access to the area.

From identification papers, one can see that an attempt of identification took place in the days immediately before the torso from Stadil was buried. Two bodies from grave no. 60 had been separated, and since none of them could be identified more than they were Americans, one was reburied in the grave no. 60 and the other removed to grave no. 96 on June 12, 1947. This grave number does not appear in the Grave Protocol or in the Church Register. Both registers have got grave number 93 as the last registered burial.

The torso was the day after – on June 13, 1947 - buried next to the unknown American airman, who the day before had been laid in the grave no. 96. The torso of the Australian airman therefore had grave no. 97. A technical, practical arrangement - but no fine and venerable funeral!

The burial plots

About 200 people lived in Svino church district at the time of the war (in 2016 there are approximately 180 inhabitants). The church could with its almost 100 seats hold about half of the parish. That means it was rather big. So was the cemetery. It had an adequate size - and a little more - compared to the population, it was supposed to cover. But it did not, however, have the capacity to be central cemetery for allied airmen crashed over the southern and western part of Zealand, Moen, Lolland and Falster with the number of funerals, this fact meant.

However it took some time before the church council became quite aware of this. The first two airmen were buried side by side in an empty grave in the middle of the cemetery one week apart in 1942. Gruber on May 13 and Gruchy on May 20, 1942. The next three airmen (Gourlay and two unknown airmen) were buried behind the church's apse – it is immediately east of the church - on Oct. 7, 1942.

Already two days later they had to find room for a further four airmen. Spowart, Higson and two unknown airmen got on October 9 burial ground immediately north of the two airmen recently buried behind the church's apse.

After only thirteen days, they had to find room for Henry from New Zealand. He got his grave in continuation west of the recently four buried.

Then the funerals took speed.

During 1943, corpses and body parts from no less than 48 allied airmen were buried in 41 graves, as some of them were buried in common graves.

Now the cemetery simply was filled.

The 48 airmen buried in 1943 have been buried in an area north of the church. An area which had been laid out as unused land, and on which the church's restrooms and fuel space were situated in the northern part of the area.

Now it was difficult to find out what to do.

An extension of the cemetery was needed.

The church council negotiated with proprietary Harald Hansen, who had a piece of land north of the church, and Reverend Lindelov wrote and applied to The Church Ministry for permission to the expansion of the cemetery.

The plot amounting 645m2 was acquired for 200kr. and was immediately fenced in roughly with laths.

The purchase price, temporary fencing, penetration and repair of curtain wall and leveling of the new land amounted to 766kr.

Bishop Axel Rosendal gave on June 23, 1944 commitment that the cost could be covered *"by either the State Treasury or from the Church Ministry as a payment from church funds,"* as he puts it.

So far so good.

During 1944, 44 allied airmen were buried in the newly acquired land.

In 1945 two airmen were buried immediately after the war (Ritchie 11.05 and Russel 10.06).

In 1946, Hall was buried on February 10, and the Irish Thornton was buried as an unknown Canadian on June 23. In 1947, the torso from Stadil was buried on June 13. By the excavations and attempt for identifying after the war there were on many occasions found more bodies or body parts in the same coffin, so the total number of buried came to be 108 allied airmen.

The reason to these surprising discoveries was that the coffins were closed when they arrived to Svino to be buried. Therefore the Reverend as well as the Gravedigger had to rely on the information, given by the Germans, about which bodies were in the various coffins - information which unfortunately was not always correct.

The graves are assembled and unknown airmen identified

A short time after the war had ended there was a strong sentiment among the local population in and around Svino that you should try to raise funds for the establishment of a memorial grove for the allied airmen.

A committee chaired by the District Governor of Praestoe County was set up, and money was collected and actually money also was granted to the project from the public treasury.

However, there were some problems related to the project, which had to be solved.

One of the problems was that the airmen had been buried on different spots at Svino cemetery, and you had to move the first buried airmen from the old cemetery to the newly dedicated part of the cemetery, if you should be able to establish a coherent memorial grove.

Reverend Johannes Lindelov wrote on April 1, 1946 to the Ministry of Ecclesiastical Affairs and asked for permission to move the 26 first buried coffins:

"The bodies are in the period: May 9, 1942 – May 13, 1943 at the request of the German Wehrmacht buried in an unused part of Svino cemetery. As the number of buried airmen over time became more than 100, a new cemetery had to be constructed. As this now is being established as a memorial grove for allied airmen, both church board as well as the allied military authorities find that it is both natural and necessary, too that the first in the northeast corner of the cemetery buried 26 coffins are moved to the new cemetery, where there is room enough for them too; in this way we can create a beautiful orderly burial of the 103 bodies, as they then can come to lie in 4 rows with 26 bodies in each row, around which the Memorial can unite in a beautiful and harmonious way; while otherwise those 26 graves will lie outside the memorial grove and in no way can be held within its framework. ".

At that time, neither Thornton nor the torso from Stadil had occurred yet, and Reverend Lindelov was not aware that the number of dead, he had registered, did not entirely agree with the actual contents of the closed coffins, which the Germans during the war had sent to burial at Svino cemetery.

Reverend Lindelov got his permission, and the first buried airmen were moved to the new cemetery - amongst those Gruber and Gruchy, the first two airmen – who according to the cemetery protocol - were buried in May 1942 in a double grave in the middle of the cemetery. But permission has been given to move 26 coffins, so they were moved too, although Reverend Lindelov had only asked for permission to move the bodies from the northeast corner of the cemetery.

A group of British military personnel from Missing Research Enquiry Service participated at the relocation of the 26 coffins.

They were interested in examining the unidentified airmen - and perhaps also the airmen identified by the Germans.

It was for good reason, as now both names and identities could be put on several of the unknown airmen. They also found out that the Germans had swapped around the identity of several of the dead airmen. Sometimes the characteristics that the Germans had tacked on one coffin belonged to quite another coffin.

The reason to these mix-ups might be that reporting sometimes came long after the dead airmen had been buried. It could also be because many dead airmen often were to be handled at the same time, and then the punctuality could obviously fail.

What were sent to Svino cemetery from the Germans could be messages like this:

"Leichenteile (Brust ohne Kopf) – unbekannt – am 26.9.42 bei Nystedt an Land geschwemt. Am 7.10 42 mit 3 in Svinö beigesetzt."

Or it could be a report as below:

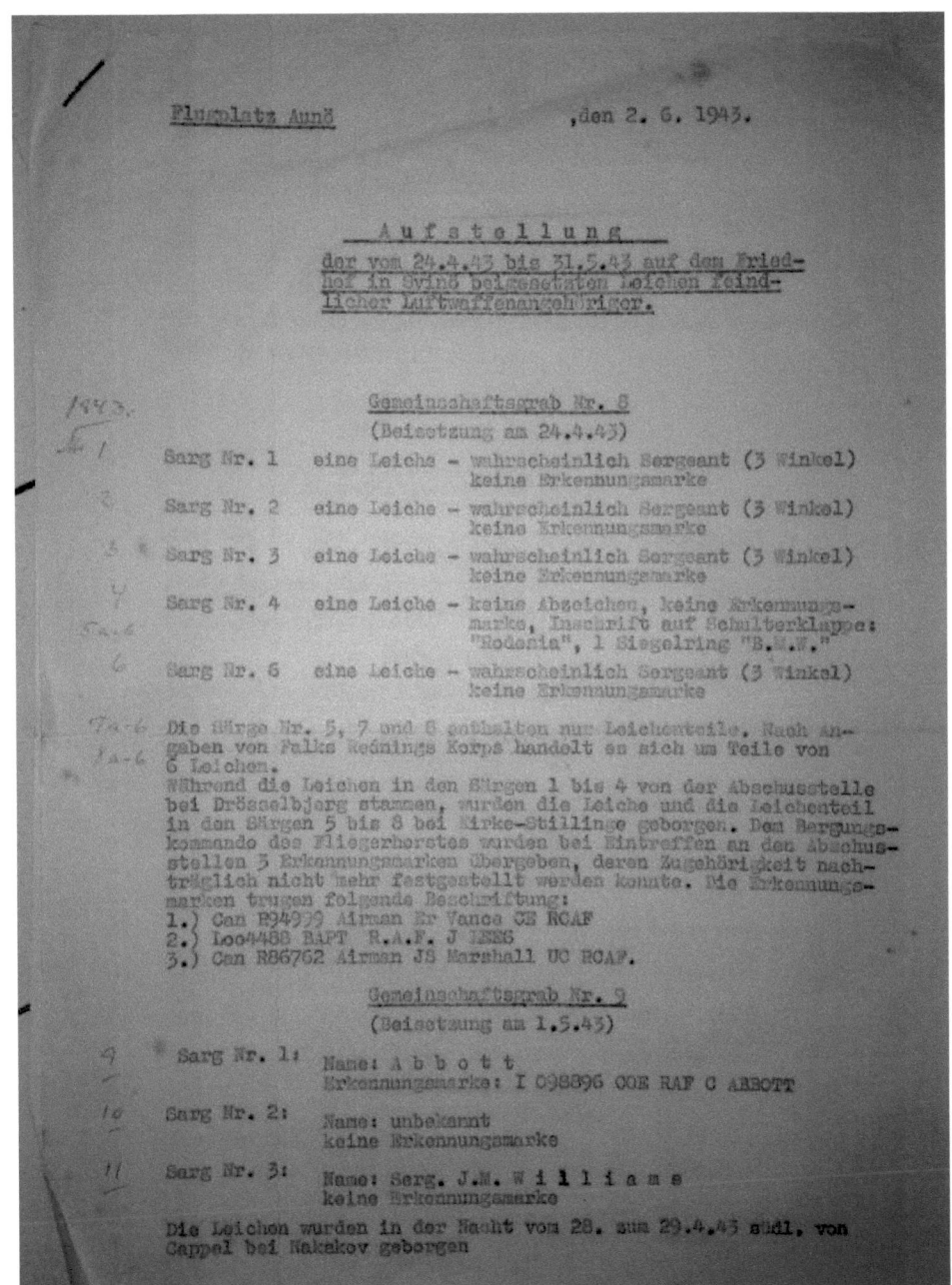

Apparently, Willis was buried in grave no. 9 in the fourth coffin arriving to be buried on April 24, 1943, as shown by the German reporting on the image.

The Germans buried him as unknown - however, characterized by a signet ring with the initials BMW and shoulder strap that read Rhodesia.

All this conformed to Willis, who came from Rhodesia and whose wife was actually named Betty. She repeatedly had traveled all the way from South Africa to visit her husband's grave - most recently in 1993, when she was here on the occasion of the 50th anniversary of the death of the spouse (thereof more p. 70). It was her initials that were engraved in the ring.

The problem was that these characteristics did not match the body in the specific coffin and grave but to the body in the grave no. 24, which was buried on May 21, 1943.

This was ascertained when Missing Research Enquiry Service opened the coffins in late April 1946

MISSING RESEARCH ENQUIRY SERVICE

Copenhagen, 3 May 1946.

Nedenstaaende fremsender vi en Fortegnelse over Allierede Flyvere begravede i Gravene Nummer I og II samt 1 til 24, idet vi henleder Deres Opmærksomhed paa, at det nu er lykkedes at fastslaa flere af de hidtil ukendte Flyveres Identitet. De bedes venligst foretage de fornødne Rettelser og Tilføjelser i Deres Register.

Fundet.		Begravet.	Navn og Detailler.	Grav Nr.
9/5/42	St. Linde Møen	18/5/42	Gruber, Engelsk Sergeant	I
16/5/42	Nr Nakskov	20/5/42	Gruchy, Sgt. 798-608	II
1/10/42	Vesteregn Langel.	7/10/42	R.J. Gourlay, CAN R105633	1
26/9/42	Nysted Lolland	7/10/42	Ukendt	1
25/9/42	Boleby Lolland	7/10/42	Ukendt	1
1/10/42	Vesteregn Langel.	9/10/42	Q. Spowart 547329	2
28/9/42	Holstenborg	9/10/42	G.W.F. Higson 1053150	3
19/10/42	Skals	22/10/42	J. Henry, Sgt. 405266	4
24/9/42	Hyldekrog	9/10/42	Ukendt Flyver-Ingeniør	5
26/9/42	Nysted Lolland	9/10/42	Ukendt Flight-Sergeant	5
21/4/43	Drösselbjerg & Kongsmark	24/4/43	F/Sgt. J.S. Marshall R86762 Sgt. D.O. Farley 1575746	6 6
21/4/43	Drösselbjerg	24/4/43	S/Ldr. K. Blake 40202 Pilot	7
21/4/43	Drösselbjerg	24/4/43	Sgt. Lees 1004486 Pilot.	8
21/4/43	Kirke Stillinge	24/4/43	D.F.R. Banks F/Lt. Parish 81927 F/O. E.R. Vance, CAN J16604	9 9 9
21/4/43	Drösselbjerg	24/4/43	Sgt. E.F. Krulicki	10
21/4/43	Drösselbjerg	24/4/43	Sgt. M. Fitzgerald 922593	11
21/4/43	Kirke Stillinge	24/4/43	Sgt-Observer H.F.D. Lay 987264	12
21/4/43	Kirke Stillinge	24/4/43	Sgt. G.W. Cole 1392074	13
29/4/43	Kappel, Nakskov	1/5/43	Sgt. J.M. Williams, Australsk Pilot	14
29/4/43	Kappel, Nakskov	1/5/43	Ukendt Pilot. Rang Pilot-Off.	15
29/4/43	Kappel, Nakskov	1/5/43	C. Abbott 1098896	15
5/5/43	Drösselbjerg	7/5/43	D.J. Donaldson 43934 F/Lt.	16
11/5/43	Kappel, Nakskov	14/5/43	J.A. Ramsay, CAN R93418	17
13/5/43	Drösselbjerg	14/5/43	Sgt. L. Whyatt 541136	18
				19

32

MISSING RESEARCH ENQUIRY SERVICE

Fundet.		Begravet.	Navn og Detailler	Grav Nr.
14/5/43	Dr Hasselbjerg	18/5/43	Ukendt	20
15/5/43	Dr Hasselbjerg	18/5/43	Jenkins	21
15/5/43	Korsør	18/5/43	Ukendt	22
18/5/43	Dr Hasselbjerg	21/5/43	W.J. Parsons 120073 F/Lt.	23
18/5/43	Dr Hasselbjerg	21/5/43	G.K. Willis 134109 F/O.	24

Hubert Brooke fil.

As shown on the document (p.32), the British military authorities write ... "*Please, make the necessary corrections and additions in Your registry.*"

However, this was not done quite consistently.

Neither grave protocol nor church register are updated with all the changes received from Missing Research Enquiry Service. A few changes have been introduced but as an example Willis is still listed in the church register as lying in tomb no.9 and in the graveyard protocol an unknown airman is still lying in grave no. 24, although the English identified Willis in this grave.

The same applies to Cross and Shogren, who during their burials seemed to have been mixed up. By exhumation and identifying, it was established that Cross actually was in the grave where Shogren was registered to be and vice versa. This has never been changed in neither the parish nor burial protocol.

The Americans were trying to identify the unknown airmen, too.

In the archive of Svino Memorial Grove you can find a letter from Major Charles J. Jorgensen, American Graves Registration Comd. Denmark Detachment, where he runs a list of exhumed, identified and reburied American airmen. The letter is dated June 14, 1947, and mentions the achievements and changes which are the result of the excavations that took place from June 9 to 12, 1947 - just before the torso from Stadil came to Svinø.

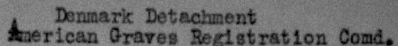

```
                        Denmark Detachment
                    American Graves Registration Comd.


                                                 Copenhagen, Denmark
                                                 14 June 1947


         Pastor Johannes Lindelov
         Kjong, Syaelland

         Dear Pastor Lindelov:

              For your information, and to assist in correcting the burial
         records for Svino church yard the following results of our work
         at Svino on 9, 10, 11, 12 of June 1947. are listed by grave
         number:

         Grave 40         No change in records
           "   43         Lt. Donald V. Scavotto - identified
           "   58         Three bodies seperated. Sgt. Gerrard Horton
                          identified and reburied alone in this grave.
           "   59         Identity of Sgt. Sheren confirmed.
           "   60         Two bodies found and seperated. One unknown
                          American reburied in this grave.
           "   62         Identity of Sgt. Schramm confirmed.
           "   68         No change in records.
           "   94         Sgt. Forrest Kayser - previously in Grave 58,
                          now reburied in Grave 94 on 12 June 1947.
           "   95         Sgt. Zvonimir P. Sambol - previously in
                          Grave 58. Now reburied in Grave 95 on 12 June 1947.
           "   96         Unknown American. Seperated from other body in
                          Grave 60 and buried seperately 12 June 1947.

              That the frequent disruption of the beautiful Svino cemetery
         is distressing to the community I am well aware. I feel certain,
         however, that you and all of your parishoners sympathize with the
         work that eventually results in identification of these dead, and
         the consequent relief of the anguish felt by parents whose sons
         disappeared so long ago.


                                        Very truly yours,



                                        CHARLES J. JORGENSEN
                                        MAJOR FA
                                        U.S. Army
```

Although both the British and Americans made an energetic attempt to identity their airmen, who were buried as unknown during the war, they did not always succeed. There are still eight unidentified airmen buried in Svino Memorial Grove, and relatives are still searching for their loved ones who perished during World War 2.

As late as in 2003, I was asked about information concerning Lt. Abernathy USAAF, as his family thought, he might have been buried as unknown at Svino cemetery in April 1944.

In flying-archaeological department in Danish Historical Flying Society they had learned that he might be one of the two unknown Americans buried in grave no. 60 in Svino Memorial Grove, one of which was exhumed and reburied in grave no. 96 in the days between the 9th and 12th of June 1947.

As stated in the letter from Major Charles J. Jorgensen, American Graves Registration Comd. Denmark Detachment, both corpses found in grave no. 60, were reburied as unknown (p.34).

One might of course have guessed that one of these Americans could be Abernathy, since there is no proof of identity for any of the two if you solely rely on Svino Church archive and protocols, but according to Anders Bjornvad in the book "Fallen allied airmen", it turned out later that the grave no. 60 contained the remains of Sgt. Edward Walter Cisek and Sgt. Fred Earnest Stilles, both USAAF SQD. 755.

This fits perfectly well with an exchange of correspondence I've had with Ferdinand M. Dèssente, Custodian Guide at Ardennes American Cemetery at Neuville-en-Condroz in Belgium, who mentions both of these airmen by name as exhumed from Svino, Denmark, and transported to Neuville-en-Condroz cemetery in Belgium along with 43 other Americans in May 1948.

Moreover, he could tell that both – according to his archives - later were sent from Neuville-en-Condroz, Belgium to the US for reburying.

The identification of Cisek and Stilles must have been made in connection with the transfer to Belgium in May 1948, and it must have taken place after the exhumation from Svino, as you in the archive of Svino Memorial Grove can find a receipt for the 45 exhumed Americans of which 4 were not identified.

Having identified Cisek and Stilles only two unknown Americans have been buried at Svino cemetery.

For the family Abernathy however, it must have been terrible not knowing where William Abernathy was buried - and if at all he had been found and buried.

Already immediately after the war his mother was searching for him. You can see this through the correspondence between Reverend Lindelov and the British authorities, found in the archive of Svino Memorial Grove, but Reverend Lindelov could not help.

Neither could I, when I was contacted in 2003, when it was his then 78-year-old sister who tried to find him.

The American airmen

Immediately after the war it was uncertain what was going to happen to the American airmen who had been buried in Europe - including in Denmark, where a total of 134 Americans had been laid to rest during the war. 46 of these Americans were buried at Svino cemetery, which therefore was that cemetery in Denmark, where most American airmen had been buried.
But what was now going to happen to them?
Should they remain where they had been buried?
Should they be assembled in each country in American war cemeteries?
Should they be exhumed and sent to the United States to be reburied at the war cemeteries over there?
Should they be exhumed and sent home to their relatives to be reburied in a cemetery near their home?

All options were apparently open, and in May 1946 the United States Public Law 383 was passed by the US Congress adopted by President Truman.
This law stated that the closest relative to an overseas buried soldier could decide whether the dead were to remain where he was buried, or he was to be exhumed to be reburied in one of the US military cemeteries, which would be established in Europe, or he should be taken home for reburying in the United States.
The unidentified American soldiers were to be gathered at US military cemeteries in Europe.
Reverend Lindelov was informed of this law in a letter from the Ministry of Foreign Affairs, dated September 14, 1946 but had nevertheless hoped that the Americans might remain at Svino, where plans for establishment of a memorial grove for the fallen airmen from World War II had already started.
In December 1946 a letter was sent to gravedigger Niels Christian Hansen from Gustave E. Weimann, Major, US Army, American Graves Registration Command, with   headquarters in Bad Sooden-Allendorf in Germany.
The letter was referring to Major Weimann's visit to Svino two weeks earlier, where the gravedigger had shown him the plans for the proposed memorial grove, and Major Weimann asks in the letter if a drawing of the planned memorial grove could be sent to him.
Whether these plans for a memorial grove have been circulated to the relatives to the American airmen so that they could decide what they wanted to happen to their dead relatives, or the plans just have been reviewed and discussed in the American Graves Registration Command is not known, but on April 26, 1948 Reverend Lindelov received a letter from Edward J. Sparks, Charge d'Affaires ad interim at the US Embassy in Copenhagen, notifying that a team from the American Graves Registration Command would arrive at Svino and exhume all the American airmen except one, according to the wishes of their relatives.
The American airmen were then to be sent home or to be reburied with other American soldiers in Europe.

Copenhagen, Denmark
26 April 1948

Hr. Sognepræst Johannes Pedersen Lindeløv
Køng, pr. Lundby
Svinø

My dear Sognepræst Lindeløv:

It is my understanding that the Danish Ministry of Ecclesiastical Affairs has already informed you with respect to the plans of my Government regarding the remains of American World War II dead, and that detachments of the United States Army's American Graves Registration Command were soon to begin operations at Svinø, to carry out the expressed wishes of the next-of-kin of these American deceased. According to the present schedule, a disinterring team of the American Graves Registration Command will arrive at Svinø on 5 May and should complete their work on 10 May.

As you may be aware, even before the conclusion of World War II, the mothers, fathers, and wives of the men of the United States who had lost their lives so far from home began to ask that the remains of their loved ones be returned to them. In response to the will of the people, the Congress of the United States enacted the necessary legislation, now known as United States Public Law 383, which was approved by President Truman in May of 1946. Pursuant to this law all next-of-kin were allowed to determine whether they desired that their deceased be returned to the United States, reburied in permanent United States World War II cemeteries to be established overseas, or remain where originally buried. By Government ruling, all unidentified American dead are to be reburied in the permanent United States military cemeteries overseas.

In accordance with this law, the next-of-kin of all United States World War II dead in Denmark were asked to express their desires. The next-of-kin of 40 of the 41 identified Americans now

37

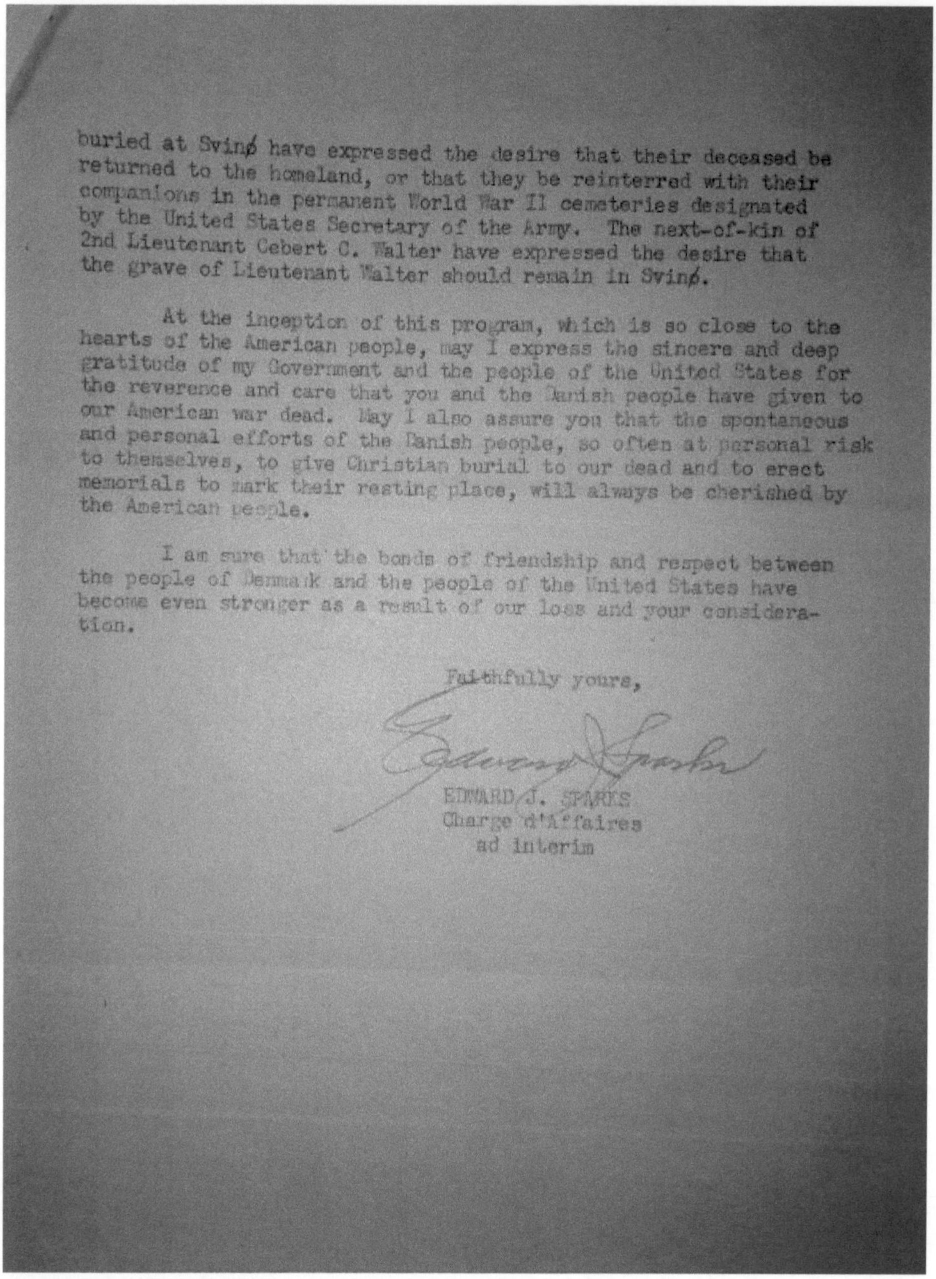

buried at Svinø have expressed the desire that their deceased be
returned to the homeland, or that they be reinterred with their
companions in the permanent World War II cemeteries designated
by the United States Secretary of the Army. The next-of-kin of
2nd Lieutenant Cebert C. Walter have expressed the desire that
the grave of Lieutenant Walter should remain in Svinø.

At the inception of this program, which is so close to the
hearts of the American people, may I express the sincere and deep
gratitude of my Government and the people of the United States for
the reverence and care that you and the Danish people have given to
our American war dead. May I also assure you that the spontaneous
and personal efforts of the Danish people, so often at personal risk
to themselves, to give Christian burial to our dead and to erect
memorials to mark their resting place, will always be cherished by
the American people.

I am sure that the bonds of friendship and respect between
the people of Denmark and the people of the United States have
become even stronger as a result of our loss and your considera-
tion.

Faithfully yours,

EDWARD J. SPARKS
Charge d'Affaires
ad interim

The airman, who in 1948 was to remain at Svino cemetery, was 2nd Lieutenant
Cebert C. Walter, whose family had wished that he should remain, where he had
been buried.

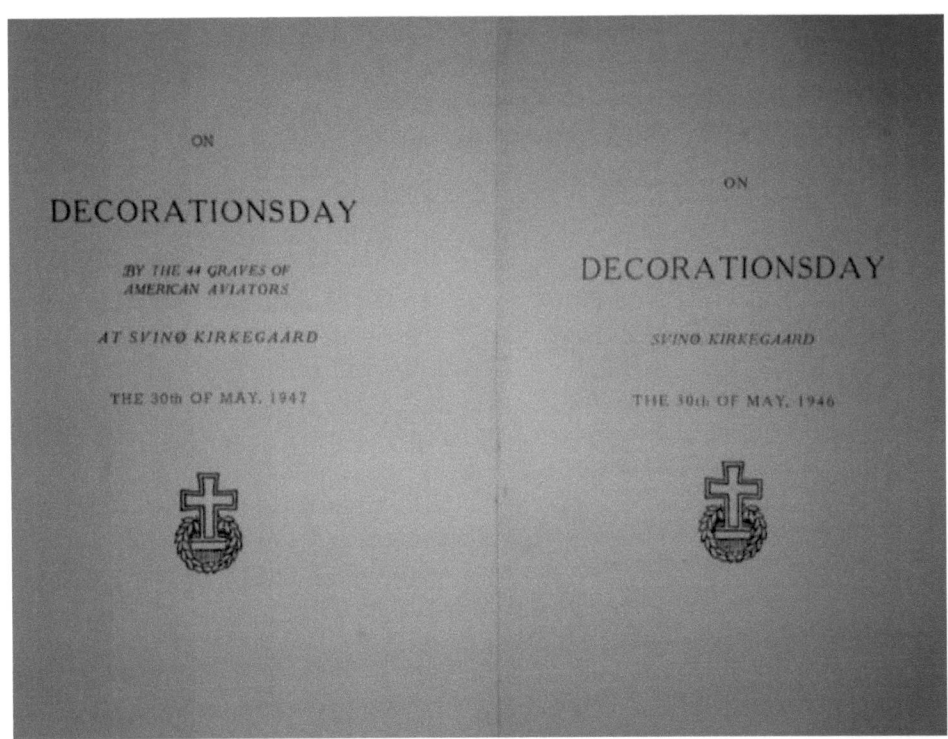

ON

DECORATIONSDAY

BY THE 44 GRAVES OF
AMERICAN AVIATORS

AT SVINØ KIRKEGAARD

THE 30th OF MAY, 1947

ON

DECORATIONSDAY

SVINØ KIRKEGAARD

THE 30th OF MAY, 1946

The exhumation of the Americans was to take place in the days from May 5th to May 10th, a rather unfortunate chosen period, as it was in these days, Denmark's Liberation day usually was celebrated.

Besides the American Decorations day May 30 had been celebrated in Svino church and Memorial Grove in both 1946 and 1947, so all together the American decision was a little contrary to wishes and praxis at Svino.

But now the American soldiers had to leave Svino, and already two years earlier - presumably in connection with the adoption of the Act in the United States about the possibility to take home the dead soldiers - the Church Ministry had sent out instructions on how this was to be done practically.

The instruction said that the place for the exhumation should be screened, but official representatives of the cemetery and of the church had the right to be present.

One had to proceed cautiously when the exhumation approached the coffin, and if the coffin was broken, the body or body parts were to be placed on a clean canvas in order to be examined to establish the identity of the deceased – if possible and if this had not been obvious.

There was also laid down guidelines for the use of disinfectants and disinfectant soap, and it was announced that it was the plan to use landing crafts from the war, located in a nearby port to take away the dead Americans.

But how many Americans were actually buried at Svino? And in which graves?

When we can ask such questions, it is because we in Svino have registered 46 buried Americans. 42 identified and four unknown, 2 of which later became known – which after that means 44 identified and 2 unknown.

But Edward J. Sparks, Charge d'Affaires ad interim at the US Embassy in Copenhagen writes in his letter from April 1948 about "40 of the 41 identified" who are to be exhumed.

Furthermore, there are three lists of exhumed US airmen in the archive of Svinø Memorial Grove, but none of the three lists are identical.

One of the lists which is a bit spotty and also undated – might be a working draft? – counts 44 exhumed Americans from Svino cemetery - three of which are unknown. Two unknown Americans are thus missing, as Donald V. Scavotto in grave no. 43 is listed as unknown.

The second list, dated May 8, 1948 and signed by Major Gustave H. Weimann, counts four unknown dead American airmen and includes Scavotto in grave no. 43. According to this list there are rightfully 45 American airmen to be exhumed in 1948.

However, there is a little awkward - but fatal - detail on this list, and that is that it says that they have exhumed Carrol G. Boyd from grave no. 72.

I hope not, for in the grave no. 72, was Canadian Rumble. Boyd was in grave no. 73. Or was he? In the parish and burial protocol Rumble actually is in grave 72, but according to CWG's register he lies in grave no. 73. But let's just hope that the right body has been exhumed together with the other Americans!

In the instructions for exhumation - also signed by Major Gustave H. Weimann and dated April 23, 1948 – it says that Boyd was exhumed from grave no. 73.

Furthermore, there is in the instructions for the exhumation mentioned four unknown (among which Gilles and Cisek later has been identified).

In the instructions for exhumation from April 1948, which lists 46 buried Americans, there is a minus with Cebert Walter's name, whose family had not wanted him exhumed, so this list seems correct.

CEMETERY	NAME	RANK	ASN	GRAVE
Svino	Anasimowicz, Joseph T.	Sgt.	33031319	83
Svino	Avantini, Carmino F.	Sgt.	12173640	55
Svino	Bastone, Pat. J.	2nd Lt.	O-768922	89
Svino	Berea, John P.	Sgt.	11095768	56
Svino	Boyd, Carall G.	1st Lt.	O-804598	73
Svino	Caldwell, Earl Jr.	S/Sgt.	3750090	86
Svino	Cantrell, William	Sgt.	38439603	70
Svino	Carrasquillo, Joe E.	S/Sgt.	12144242	47
Svino	Cavanaugh, Walter V.	2nd Lt.	O-735172	45
Svino	Craighead, William H.	2nd Lt.	O-682008	76
Svino	Cummings, Herbert E.	S/Sgt.	3437721	87
Svino	Davis, Thomas J.	S/Sgt.	35420888	85
Svino	Derochan, John A.	Sgt.	39549202	78
Svino	Gorgon, Frank	Sgt.	16113758	79
Svino	Haney, Wilbur, L.	2nd Lt.	O-689234	52
Svino	Horner, Clentis L.	Sgt.	18220787	53
Svino	Horten, Gerrard	Sgt.	18176834	58
Svino	Huffman, Billy L.	2nd Lt.	O-877280	48
Svino	Jensen, Henry J.	S/Sgt.	39551854	67
Svino	Kayser, Forest	Sgt.	35044785	58
Svino	Larton, Edward A.	2nd Lt.	O-731386	36
Svino	Lewis, Edwin R.	2nd Lt.	O-663927	38
Svino	Martinez, Albert E.	Sgt.	38380252	49
Svino	Massoy, James Y.	2nd Lt.	O-748434	54
Svino	Mulhearn, Paul Jr.	Sgt.	31303563	71
Svino	Myers, Edward A.	S/Sgt.	32385808	39
Svino	Oxrider, George J.	Major	O-435983	80
Svino	Pinning, Charles B.	1st Lt.	O-798575	44
Svino	Plynell(stmny)Donald J.	2nd Lt.	O-692457	51
Svino	Pyrz, Joseph T.	Sgt.	36340060	57
Svino	Quinlan, Johnny	2nd Lt.	O-738574	50
Svino	Raley, Raymond K.	S/Sgt.	18162612	61
Svino	Samuel, Evonisir P.	Sgt.	36735309	58
Svino	Schramm John H.	Sgt.	31254148	62
Svino	Snoren, Sidney	S/Sgt.	32814617	59
Svino	Thiem, Walter J.	1st Lt.	O-063431	41
Svino	Tomor, Edward H.	2nd Lt.	O-680769	46
Svino	Tomlinson, George B.	2nd Lt.	O-751774	75
Svino	Walter, C. C.	2nd Lt.	O-734040	42
Svino	Maluck, Adolph	Sgt.	8147823	81
Svino	Wilkinson, Richard L.	T/Sgt.	35259717	35
Svino	Unknown			60
Svino	Unknown			43
Svino	Unknown			40

This photo shows the undated list of exhumed American airmen from Svino cemetery. But two unknown airmen are missing, and furthermore Scavotto in grave no. 43 is listed as unknown

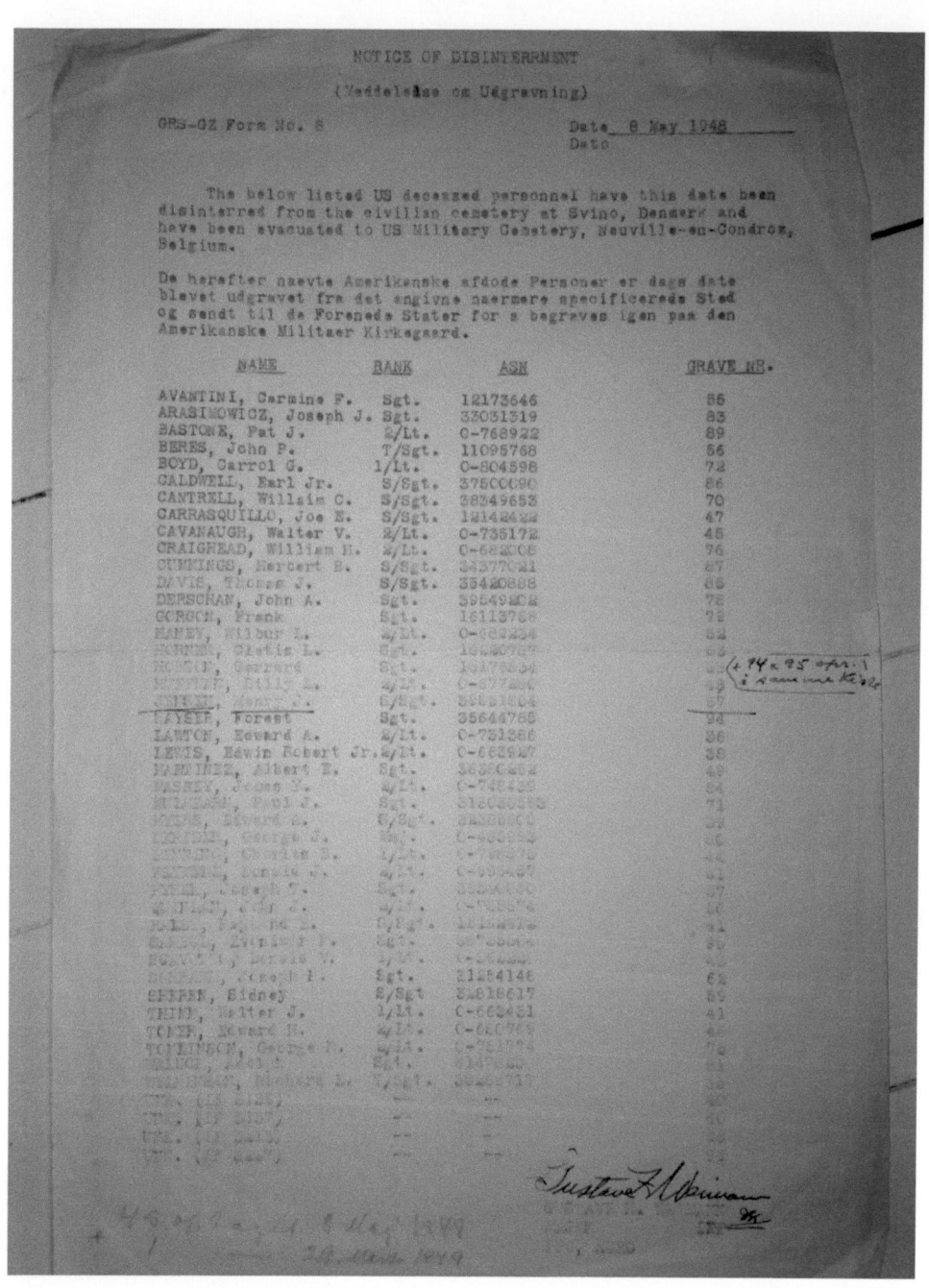

NOTICE OF DISINTERRMENT

(Meddelelse om Udgrevning)

GRS-GZ Form No. 8   Date 8 May 1948
                                      Dato

The below listed US deceased personnel have this date been
disinterred from the civilian cemetery at Svino, Denmark and
have been evacuated to US Military Cemetery, Neuville-en-Condroz,
Belgium.

De herefter naevte Amerikanske afdøde Personer er dags dato
blevet udgravet fra det angivne naermere specificerede Sted
og sendt til de Forenede Stater for a begraves igen paa den
Amerikanske Militaer Kirkegaard.

NAME	RANK	ASN	GRAVE NR.
AVANTINI, Carmine F.	Sgt.	12173646	85
ARASIMOWICZ, Joseph J.	Sgt.	33031319	83
BASTONE, Pat J.	2/Lt.	O-768922	89
BERES, John P.	T/Sgt.	11095768	55
BOYD, Carrol G.	1/Lt.	O-804598	72
CALDWELL, Earl Jr. C.	S/Sgt.	37500090	86
CANTRELL, William C.	S/Sgt.	38349653	70
CARRASQUILLO, Joe E.	S/Sgt.	19142422	47
CAVANAUGH, Walter V.	2/Lt.	O-735172	45
CRAIGHEAD, William H.	2/Lt.	O-682008	76
CUMMINGS, Herbert B.	S/Sgt.	34377021	87
DAVIS, Thomas J.	S/Sgt.	35420888	88
DERSCHAN, John A.	Sgt.	39549202	78
GOROCH, Frank	Sgt.	16113768	73
HANEY, Wilbur L.	2/Lt.	O-682354	82
	Sgt.		
	Sgt.		
	4/Lt.		
	T/Sgt.		
LAYSIE, Forest	Sgt.	35644765	94
LAWTON, Edward A.	2/Lt.	O-751286	96
LEWIS, Edwin Robert Jr.	2/Lt.	O-663947	38
MARTINEZ, Albert E.	Sgt.	36800482	49
	4/Lt.		84
	Sgt.		71
	S/Sgt.		
	Sgt.		
	1/Lt.		
	4/Lt.		
	Sgt.		
	4/Lt.		
	T/Sgt.		
	Sgt.		
	4/Lt.		
	Sgt.	31254146	61
SPEREN, Sidney	S/Sgt.	32618617	59
THUM, Walter J.	1/Lt.	O-663431	41
TONER, Edward E.	4/Lt.	O-680765	
TOMLINSON, George H.	4/Lt.	O-751274	74
	Sgt.		
	T/Sgt.		

This list shows the correct number of exhumed Americans, but Boyd seems to be in grave no. 72 and not in 73

Operational Instructions (No. D-29)   25 April 1945.

The following list of U.S. Military Deceased will be disinterred
and evacuated to U.S. Military Cemetery, Neuville en Condros, Belg.

SVING Cemetery

					Grave
1.	ARASIMOWICZ, JOSEPH J%	Sgt	33031319		52
2.	AVANTI, CARMINE F.	Sgt	12173646	F	55
3.	BASTONE, PAT J%	2nd Lt	0-768922	"	56
4.	BURRS, JOHN P.	T/Sgt	11095768	"	45
5.	BOYD, CAROLL G%	1st Lt	0-804598	"	55
6.	CALDWELL, EARL JR.	S/Sgt	37500090	"	70
7.	CANTRELL, WILLIAM O.	S/Sgt	38439655	"	47
8.	CARRASQUILLO, JOE R.	S/Sgt	12142422	"	45
9.	CAVANAUGH, WALTER V.	2nd Lt	0-735172	"	76
10.	CRAIGHEAD, WILLIAM H%	2nd Lt	0-682008	"	87
11.	CUMMINGS, HERBERT B.	S/Sgt	34577021	"	85
12.	DAVIS, THOMAS J.	S/Sgt	35420898	"	76
13.	IBRSCHAN, JOHN A.	Sgt	39549202	"	79
14.	GORGON, FRANK	Sgt	16113759	"	52
15.	HANNY, WILBUR L.	2nd Lt	0-699854	"	64
16.	HOHMER, CLETIS L.	Sgt	15820797	"	64
17.	HORTON, GERRARD	Sgt	18176834	"	66
18.	HUFFMAN, BILLY L.	2nd Lt	0-677230	"	44
19.	JENSEN, HENRY J.	S/Sgt	39551364	"	67
20.	KAYNER, FOREST	Sgt	36644795	"	94
21.	LAWTON, EDWARD A.	2nd Lt	0-731594	"	54
22.	LEWIS, EDWIN R. JR.	2nd Lt	0-265927	"	59
23.	MARTINEZ, ALBERT E%	Sgt	35590656	"	49
24.	MASSEY, JAMES Y.	2nd Lt	0-743430	"	54
25.	MULBRANN, PAUL J%	Sgt	35305566	"	72
26.	MYERS, EDWARD A.	W/Sgt	35235606	"	59
27.	OURIER, GEORGE J%	Major	0-433959	"	60
28.	PINNING, CHARLES R.	1st Lt	0-795578	"	44
29.	PLYMELL, DONALD S%	T/Sgt	0-692457	"	53
30.	PERRE, JOSEPH T.	Sgt	35740066	"	57
31.	QUINLAN, JOHN J.	Sgt	0-735874	"	50
32.	RAINY, RAYMOND R.		31560534	"	51
33.	SAMBOL, EVONIMIR T.		35093364	"	93
34.	SCAVOTTO, EDWARD N.	1st Lt	0-0	"	43
35.	SCHRANN, JOHN E.	Sgt		"	62
36.	SHERER, AIMECK			"	41
37.	THIMM, WALTER C.	2nd Lt	0-590769	"	46
38.	TOMER, EDWARD H.	2nd Lt	0-731774	"	73
39.	TOMLINSON, GEORGE R.	2nd Lt	0-736866	"	48
40.	WALTHER, ORBERT G.	S/Sgt	6147333	"	91
41.	WALUCK, ADOLPH	S/Sgt		"	35
42.	WILKINSON, RICHARD L.	T/Sgt	35250717	"	48
43.	UNKNOWN (IF-3139)	--	---		
44.	UNKNOWN (IF-3137)	--	----	Grave	60
45.	UNKNOWN (IF-3213)	--	----	"	65 A
46.	UNKNOWN (IF-3227)	--	----	"	66 A

GUSTAVE E% WEIMANN
Major   Inf.

This is to certify that the above listed graves have been disinterred.

In this instruction for exhumation, which is rather blurred, Boyd is in grave no. 73, Scavotto in grave no. 43 is also listed by name. Furthermore there are four unknown American airmen.

At first the 45 exhumed airmen were taken to the American cemetery in the Ardennes in Belgium near the city of Neuville-en-Condroz not far from Liege.

From here two were sent to Luxembourg and reburied there:
Edwin R. Lewis og Cletis Horner

30 were sent to the United States and reburied there:
Walter J.Thimm, Richard L.Wilkinson, Edward A. Myers, Joseph J. Arasimowicz, Joseph E. Carrasquillo, Edward H. Tomer, Walter V. Cavanaugh, Charles B. Pinning, Billy L. Huffman, Gerrard Horton, Forest E. Kayser, Edward Walter Cisek, Fred Earnest Stilles, Sidney Sheren, Wilbur L. Haney, John J. Quinlan, John P. Beres Jr., Albert E. Martinez, Joseph T. Pyrek, William C. Cantrell, Carroll G. Boyd, Henry J. Jensen, Paul J. Mulhearn, John A. Derschan, Pat J. Bastone, Herbert B. Cummings, Earl Caldwell Jr., Donald V. Scavotto, George E. Tomlinson, Thomas J. Davis Jr.

11 identified and two unknown were reburied at Neuville-en-Condroz- cemetery, Ardennes:
Carmine P. Avantini, William H. Craigheard, Frank Gorgon, Edward A. Lawton, James Y. Massey, Donald J. Plymell, Zvonimir L. Waist Sambol, Raymond E. Raley, John Schramm, George J. Oxrider, Adolph Waluck.

In the autumn 1994, I went to the Ardennes American Cemetery in order to find "my dead Americans." I had brought with me photocopies from the church register of Svino and thought that it might be difficult to find them amongst so many fellow countrymen, but that the task would be as daunting, as it turned out to be, I was not prepared for. More than 5,300 Americans are buried at this cemetery.
Luckily I met a very enthusiastic and knowledgeable custodian, Ferdinand M. Dessente.
Ferdind M. Dessente took his time, not only to help looking in several records in order to find my Americans, he also went on working on the case, after I had left and sent me for Christmas friendly Christmas greetings together with lists of the Americans exhumed from Svino together with information on, where they had been reburied and which of them were reburied in the Ardennes.
In addition, he sent descriptions of their aircrafts, and told me with pride that "my Americans" belonged to "The Mighty Eight".
During my visit to the Ardennes we also together found out that Anders Bjornvad was right, when he reported that there is a sort of "Denmark-row" in the American cemetery of Ardennes, as many of the Americans exhumed from Denmark are reburied in row No. 39.
But what happened to our last American airman, who was not exhumed in 1948, Cebert Walter?
Well, his family had initially not wanted him removed. But the family had also lost Cebert's brother, Harry, in the war, and when they understandably therefore wanted the two brothers buried in the same cemetery, this could be possible at the American cemetery, Magraaten, in the Netherlands.
Although the family at first had not wanted Cebert Walter exhumed, when the other Americans were exhumed from Svino, they subsequently already in December 1948 expressed a wish that they would have Cebert Walter exhumed from Denmark.
The permission was given from both the Ministry of Health as well as from The Ministry for Ecclesiastical Affairs, and on March 29, 1949 Cebert Walter was exhumed from Svino cemetery and initially taken to the Ardennes, Neuville en

Condroz, Belgium, and from here sent to Magraaten, Netherlands to be reburied near his brother.

The two brothers are not buried exactly next to one another but rather close in row 19 in Section N at the American Cemetery Magraaten, Netherlands.

According to Anders Bjornvad in the book 'Fallen airmen' eight American airmen are still buried in Denmark - but none at Svino cemetery anymore.

During the exhumation of the American airmen from Svino some gaps emerged in the otherwise uniform landscaped 4 rows of graves of allied airmen. That irritated Reverend Lindelov, and it also irritated him that the Americans at the exhumation made a mess at the cemetery. However, in spite of the asymmetric gaps between the remaining British graves, no more airmen, however, were to be exhumed and removed, so the gaps in the rows were allowed to be as they were.

In remembrance of the 46 Americans who were buried at Svino, a monument was erected in 1964 telling:

"46 American airmen fallen in World War 2 lay buried at Svino Memorial Grove in the years 1943-1948".

When the monument for the American airmen was not installed until 1964, it was because of different opinions on the monument's appearance and location.

This is evidenced by the correspondence stored in the archive of the Memorial Grove, between the Church Council, Ministry for Ecclesiastical Affairs, Ministry of Foreign Affairs and the US authorities.

In 1998 Ejvind Friis Jensen, Kvislemark, pointed out to me that in 1995 a monument was raised by veterans from the Danish association "Fight for Freedom" at Arlington National Cemetery, United States, to commemorate all American airmen who have been buried in Denmark during the war and until they had been exhumed.

The monument at Arlington cemetery was unveiled on May 10, 1995 by HRH Prince Joachim.

Svino Memorial Grove and CWGC

The transfer of Alexander Henry Hall's body from Airfield Avno to Svino Cemetery in February 1946, and the removal of the 26 coffins from the original cemetery to the new cemetery to the north were the beginning of establishing Svino Memorial Grove. Another beginning was the constitution of a committee whose job was to establish the Memorial Grove for allied airmen at Svino cemetery.

Many and also good plans were put on the table, but the case was continually delayed by the uncertainty on what was going to happen to the American airmen and also by the attempts of identifying the airmen, buried as unknown. It was a laborious process that took its time.

The committee worked however steady alongside with these challenges.

More land was bought, so a paved road to the memorial grove could be established, and plans were made regarding planting in the area and also ideas of a design for a monument appeared. They applied for financial help from the public treasury to the project through the Ministry of Ecclesiastical Affairs, but much was still uncertain.

Til

K o m i t e e n

for Anlæggelsen af en M i n d e l u n d

for de paa Svinø Kirkegaard begravede faldne allierede Flyvere

v/ Herr Amtsmand G.T o f t, Næstved.

I Fortsættelse af tidligere Drøftelser vedrørende Indretningen af
en Mindelund paa Svinø Kirkegaard for de her begravede 104 faldne allierede Flyvere og under Henvisning til,at der if.Skr.fra Kirkeministeri-
et af 26.Marts d.A.paa Finansloven før 1947/48 til dette Formaal er be-
vilget et Beløb,svarende til.Halvdelen af de med Mindelundens Anlæg m.m
forbundne Udgifter,dog ikke udover 25.000 Kr.,skal Svinø Menighedsraad
herved tillade os at meddele den høje Komite,at Menighedsraadet allere-
de -i H.t.Kirkeministeriets Tilladelse- har ladet udføre følgende Arbejder,der har medført følgende Udgifter:

Køb af Jord til Kirkegaardsudvidelse til Mindelunden.. Kr.1480,00.
Landinspektør,Mæde m.m......   - 320,00.
Indhegning -med Granitmur- af Arealet:
1.Arbejdet med Nedtagning af gl.Mur,Støbning af Fun-
    dament og Genopførelse af den ny Mur........ - 6500,00.
2.Yderligere Materialer til Murens Opførelse........... - 2200,00.
3.Medhjælperløn,Kørsel m.m................................ - 1800,00.
Flytning af 25 Kister fra midlertidig Plads til den
    øvrige store Begravelsesplads...................... - 1800,00.
Midlertidig Anlæggelse af Begravelsespladsen m.m. .... - 353,00.
                                      14453,00

Menighedsraadet har endvidere indhentet Tilbud paa følgende
Arbejder,som Tilbuddene herved fremsendes,og som det er nød-
vendigt at udføre snarest,da det ellers ikke vil kunne lade
sig gøre i Løbet af Sommeren:

I Anlæg af en befæstet Vej fra Indkørselen op til Kirken Kr.4900,00.
II Indsættelsen af en trefløjet Jern-Gitterlaage v.Indgg. - 2000,00.
III Fjernelsen af tidligere-paa Mindelundens Plads beligg., -
    og Genopførelse andetsteds af Toilet-og Brændselsrum - 2500,00.
Ledelse af Arbejderne,Tilsyn,Regnskab m.m.   - 1000,00.
                           Ialt   Kr.   24853,00.

Hvilket herved meddeles den høje Komite til
    forventet Godkendelse.

     Svinø Menighedsraad   P. M.s V.
      d.22.April 1947.

                            Johns.P.Lindeløv.
                            Fmd.,Sognepr.

When the American airmen in 1948 and 1949 had been exhumed, it became clear
that the memorial grove now was to be a solely British cemetery, and soon it was no
longer the local committee who could decide the design of Svinø Memorial Grove,
for now Commonwealth War Graves Commission took over, and the design of the
memorial grove therefore had to be similar to British military cemeteries throughout
the world.

The headstones were to be identical - the typical white "headstones".

Moreover, the British monument "Cross of Sacrifice" was put up at the cemetery, and the Commonwealth War Graves Commission would henceforward take care of the cemetery.

Commonwealth War Graves Commission was established in 1917 on the initiative of Sir Fabian Ware, and the following year 587.000 graves were registered. Three of the great architects from that time, Sir Edwin Lutyens, Sir Herbert Baker and Sir Reginald Blomfield, undertook to design and construct the many cemeteries, and also the director of the British Museum, Sir Frederic Kenyon was involved in the work. The author Rudyard Kipling was literary adviser regarding inscriptions.

The graves in Commonwealth cemeteries are arranged in rows with identical white headstones and the area between the graves are often laid out with grass.

It is a basic principle that the dead persons are buried side by side regardless of rank, race or religion.

At burial sites with more than 40 graves the monument Cross of Sacrifice is set up.

Commonwealth War Graves Commission takes the responsibility to mark and maintain the graves of the military personnel who died during the two world wars, and who came from a Commonwealth member country (Australia, Britain, Canada, India, New Zealand and South Africa).

The cost of all this is paid by the Commonwealth member countries in a proportion based on the number of these countries' graves.

The organization is now responsible for 1.7 million graves spread over 23.000 cemeteries in 154 countries worldwide.

The monument Cross of Sacrifice which can be found at Commonwealth cemeteries throughout the World.

48

The opening of Svino Memorial Grove

In early 1950, the English headstones and monuments came to Denmark, and Svino Memorial Grove could now have its final appearance.

They managed to have The Memorial Grove ready at the last minute before May 5th 1950, which was the date scheduled for the opening, to which relatives of the airmen had been invited to participate.

The opening day became a glorious day.

It was attended by 42 relatives of airmen, buried at Svino Memorial Grove.

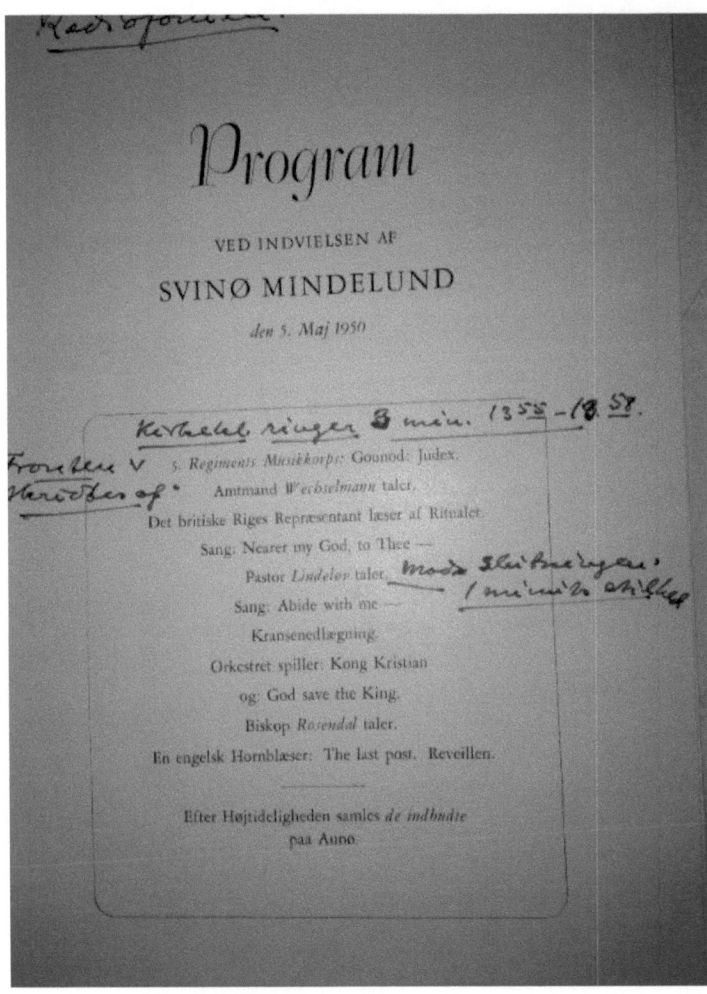

Wives, mothers, fathers, children, brothers and sisters of the dead airmen came to Denmark on this occasion. Moreover, official representatives from Britain, as well as the prefect Wechelmann from Praestoe county and Bishop Rosendal, Roskilde diocese participated and helped to make the day extra festive. Both "King Kristian" and "God Save the Queen" were to be sung and also hymns in both Danish and English

The above photo shows the program for the opening of Svino Memorial Grove, bearing Reverend Lindelov's notes on it.

Both photos above are from the opening of Svino Memorial Grove

Many Danish homes had offered accommodation to the many foreign guests, and at Airbase Avno a social gathering for several hundreds of people took place after the opening ceremony.

		SVINO CEMETERY		ACCEPTANCES 40
Name of visitor.	Profession	Name of Deceased	Relationship
Mr Joseph Abbott	Civil Servant	Sgt. C.Abbott	Father
Mrs Grace Abbott	Housewife		Mother
Mr Charles Farley	Grinder	Sgt.D. Farley	Father
Mrs Nellie Farley	Housewife		Mother
Mr Albert Russell	Grocer	Sgt.R.Russell	Father
Mrs Caroline Russell	Housewife		Mother
Mr Harold Fenton	Clerk	Sgt.G.Higson	H/Father
Mrs Ellen Fenton	Housewife		Mother nee Higson
Mr William Banks	Storeman	Sgt.D.Banks	Father
Mrs Laura Banks	Housewife		Mother
Mr William Sykes	Manager	F/Sgt.Sykes	Father
Mrs Alice Sykes	Housewife		Mother
Mr Henry Loverock	Storeman	Sgt.Loverock	Father
Mrs.Florence Loverock	Housewife		Mother
Mrs Kathleen Donaldson		F/Lt.Donaldson	Wife
Master D. Donaldson	Schoolboy		Son (11 yrs)
Mrs Mary Offen	Housewife	Sgt.F.Offen	Wife
Miss Mavis Offen	Schoolgirl		Daughter(13 yrs)
Mrs Betty Willis	Housewife	F/O.G.Willis	Wife
Mrs Margaret Lay	Housewife	Sgt.E.Lay	Wife
Mrs Elsy Lindrea	Housewife	Sgt.Lindrea	Mother
Miss Jane Lindrea	Schoolteacher		Sister
Mrs Mary Jones	Telephone Op.	Sgt.G.Jones	Sister
Mrs Jane Jones	Housewife		Mother
Mrs Harriett Hall	Housewife	F/O A.Hall	Mother
Mrs Eileen Cocale	Housewife		Sister
Mrs Sarah Woplin	Housewife	Sgt.Woplin	Mother
Mrs Gwendoline Jones	Housewife		Sister
Mrs Jane Spewart	Housewife	Sgt.G.Spewart	Mother
Miss Spewart	Sgt.W.R.A.F.		Sister
Mrs Henrietta Glendinning	Housewife	Sgt.Glendinning	Wife
Mr James Lees	Pensioner	Sgt. J. Lees	Father
Mrs Laura Rushten	Clerk		Sister
Mrs Doris Cole	Secretary	Sgt.W.Cole	Wife
Miss Doris Hoare	Civil Servant		Friend N.O.R.
Mrs Violet Whyatt	Housewife	F/Sgt.Whyatt	Sister
Mrs Helena Roobuck	Housewife		Sister in Law
Mrs Dorothy Aubrey	Secretary	F/Lt.Parsons	Sister(Parsons)
Mr Eric Aubrey	Stressman		Bro.in Law O/R
Mrs Warren	Salvation Army Officer (Female)		
Mr W.M.Burrows	(Male)		

O/R. denotes the only relatives available to make the visit.
N.O.R. denotes that there is no other relative.
N.b.

On the above shown list you can see that relatives to approximately one third of the allied airmen buried at Svino were present at the opening of the memorial grove. You can also see which relationship the representatives had to the airmen. Furthermore Reverend Lindelov has written, where the guests were to stay. You can see that also Herlufsholm Boarding school, the estate of Ohjerggaard in Kong, Airbase Avno and the estate of Rosenfeldt near Vordingborg (Oxholm) have offered accommodation to the relatives.

After the opening Reverend Lindelov received a lot of thank you letters, in which the relatives expressed their gratitude to the Danish hospitality. They had also felt how committed and compassionate the Danes were.

These letters of thanks were sent with Danish translation via the British Embassy to Reverend Lindelov.

And Reverend Lindelov was proud and happy.

The vicar and the organ player

Reverend Lindelov worked tirelessly as a vicar in Kong and Svino parish during the war.

After the war he also assisted so far, it was at all possible for him, with the help and assistance to the British and American authorities, and he corresponded with many relatives to the airmen buried at Svino cemetery.

As it was forbidden to conduct the funerals of the allied airmen, it was not without risk that he, nevertheless defied the German command, and together with the congregation went out to the cemetery after the Sunday service to officiate the graveside ceremony in order to give all the dead airmen a Christian burial, even though they had just been buried in the past week by the Germans.

Without trying to shake his meritorious work, however, an image of Reverend Lindelov as a bit of a "parish king" appears when reading his various papers and letters in the archive of Svino Memorial Grove. His descriptions of the events concerning Svino Memorial Grove at times seem quite heroic - what they, however, probably also in many cases were.

Lindelov does not put his light under a bushel - and probably in most cases rightly so.

But it the archive of The Memorial Grove you can also find a proposal for compensation for the care of the German Refugees Graves at an inappropriate large amount. Lindelov suggests that 1200kr per year would be an appropriate amount for the German government to pay to Svino Church Council for the care of refugees graves.

There are also in the archive drafts of a bill to the US authorities for the damage they have caused on Svino Memorial Grove during the exhumation of their dead airmen, which might seem a bit unreasonable when the American airmen, after all, had lost their lives for the sake of our freedom.

But was Lindelov perhaps also a little scared and maybe stubborn on some points? When I allow myself to ask this question it is because I was contacted by some family members of Jens Thomas Jensen, who was organ player at Kong and Svino churches during the war.

Jens Thomas Jensen was more than organ player. He was also a teacher and linguist and interested in English and German language and culture.

He got on with the Germans and worked as an interpreter for them.

It had of course consequences for him after the war, where both he and his then 17 years old son was picked up and accused of working for the occupying power. He had several years in prison, after which he moved to Copenhagen and worked with translation there. His wife had a mental breakdown, and the family was completely destroyed - a family that also included a resistance fighter, so there was a deep split in the poor family.

However, what was told to me independently by both family members to Jens Thomas Jensen, was that they as children during the war had overheard a telephone conversation between Jens Thomas Jensen and Reverend Lindelov.

In this telephone conversation Jens Thomas Jensen was trying to persuade Reverend Lindelov to attend the burial of the airmen, what Reverend Lindelov apparently did not want to.

Now, however, it is unknown, at what time during the war, this telephone conversation took place.

Was it in the beginning of the war, where the German chaplain conducted the burial of the airmen - that is in the period between spring 1942 and spring of 1943 - and was it perhaps Jens Thomas Jensen's business, getting Pastor Lindelov to be present together with the German chaplain at the funerals, and was it perhaps what the Reverend Lindelov did not want to?

Or did the phone call take place in the spring of 1943, when the German chaplain asked Reverend Lindelov to take over the funerals of the airmen, so he himself did not have to travel from Copenhagen to Svino to conduct funerals, and was it perhaps this, Reverend Lindelov did not want to?

Or did the phone call take place in the spring of 1944, when it has been forbidden to conduct the funerals of the airmen, and could it be that the organ player tried to convince the vicar that he had to officiate the grave side ceremony to the airmen buried by the Germans, so that all the dead airmen were given a Christian burial?

From the information I have received on the organ player together with the picture that emerges from Reverend Lindelov, when I have been reading in the material from the archive of Svino Memorial Grove, I am inclined to think that it is the second option that is the right one.

I can very well imagine that Reverend Lindelov could be so stubborn and dismissive towards the Germans that he would not take over the funerals of the airmen, solely because it was the Germans who asked him to do so.

It might be very possible that a discussion with the organ player had to take place in order to make the vicar collecting himself a little in his stubbornness and reconsider his rejection of the German proposal.

We cannot know for sure which of the above options might be the right one, but in any case the organ player Jens Thomas Jensen obtains a bit satisfaction, because he argued for the fact that all allied airmen were to have a Christian burial, involving a Danish vicar as they were buried in Danish soil.

Reverend Lindelov himself is mentioning organ player Jens Thomas Jensen in a report to Roskilde Diocese of conditions in Kong-Svino Parish on September 28, 1945.
His writes:

"Well, in the parish we did have a teacher who took service at Airbase Avno as interpreter, etc. He was also organ player at Svino Church; and of course it was neither pleasant nor soothingly; but we don't think he did inform against us. Now it

is worst for himself. Some young people went to work on Airbase Avno; but must of course also now suffer for it. "

The graves of the German refugees.

Next to Airbase Avno there was in the last year of the war and immediate after the war a refugee camp for about 1000 German refugees.

Reverend Lindelov writes that one male child was born, and 17 people died - mainly children and a few old ones.

A German vicar was in charge of the funerals, and birth registration as well as the death registrations came to Reverend Lindelov with scanty information.

The deaths took place in the last days of the war and immediately after the war. But then the refugee camp at Avno was dissolved, and the refugees were sent to other, larger camps and then home.

This fact also explains the relatively low number of dead persons.

The 17 dead German refugees were buried at Svino cemetery in the area immediately east of what is now Svino Memorial Grove. The area is currently laid out as a lawn.

The 17 graves were adorned with white-painted wooden crosses on which the name and birth and death dates of the deceased were written.

The archive of Svino Memorial Grove contains a list of the dead Germans, their birth - and death dates and also cause of death.

They all died in the period from April to July 1945 and the causes of death are pneumonia, heart weakness, kidney inflammation etc. A child also died as a result of exhaustion because of the lack of nutrition.

It is sad reading and expresses the war's cruelty – also elsewhere than among warriors.

There has not been made any great necropolis for the refugees, but their graves have been looked after and taken care of on a proper way.

In autumn 1965, the German refugees were exhumed. Of this there is an acknowledgment in the archive of the memorial grove.

In the same way as Svino cemetery was central cemetery for allied airmen, several Danish cemeteries were later made central cemeteries for German refugees.

One of these was the nearby Kastrup cemetery. Another was Vordingborg cemetery. One might therefore imagine that the German refugees from Svino had been reburied at one of these two cemeteries. However, none of them have received dead Germans in 1965, in which year the exhumation from Svino took place.

The receipt from the exhumation of the German refugees does not record where they were taken, so they might as well have been sent to Germany and reburied there.

May 4th at Svino

In the early postwar years, the American "Decorations Day" was celebrated at Svino, and it is very possible that the Danish liberation day May 4th (in the evening) and May 5th was celebrated, too.

Next, the opening of the Memorial Grove on May 5th, 1950 after all was a big event, but if May 4th and 5th subsequently has been consistently celebrated in Svino Church and Memorial Grove is a little uncertain.

During the 1970s, Mogens Gatswiller from Slagelse, however, became aware of Svino Memorial Grove and took the initiative to celebrate The Danish Liberation Day there. He was a member of a club (St. George' society) in Skelskoer, which thus became involved in the arrangement of the commemoration at Svino.

In some years the then dean Balslev from Praestoe also conducted a church service in the beginning of the event, but it was not until the early 1980s that The May 4th Ceremony found its solid form. At that time, the association 'Defend Denmark' took over responsibility for the event, and my predecessor in the ministry, Kirsten Moerch-Nielsen, who was vicar of Kong and Svino from 1982-89, was more than willing to help at the event and conduct the initial worship in Svino Church.

When I became vicar of Kong and Svino in 1989, The May 4th Ceremony was all going smooth.

The practical coordinator was Lt. Col. Donald Thestrup, head of the Air Base Avno. When airbase Avno closed in 1993, and Donald Thestrup had retired, he still continued to lead the event, now as a representative of 'Defend Denmark'.

When 'Defend Denmark' became part of the 'People and Defense', and 'People and Defense' then became 'People and Security', Donald Thestrup continued to be the practical organizer of the May 4 event right up until 2015, when the retired Colonel Bjarne Hesselberg took over.

It was - and is - a great job to make it all hang together.

Representatives of the respective embassies, soldiers associations, Home Guard, mayors, etc. are to be invited. Nobody must be forgotten. Loudspeaker systems for the cemetery have to be organized and flowers and candles at the graves. Moreover, an agreement with the Danish Air Force on the ceremonial flying formation has to be made.

Until the closure of Airbase Avno it was flying students from there, who made the ceremonial flyover, "Lost Pilot", where four small training aircrafts are flying over Svino cemetery in a special formation. Exactly above the cemetery one of the aircrafts undertakes a 'loop' to symbolize the downed airmen. The three other aircrafts continue unaffected. After a moment, the planes return and fly over the cemetery one more time. At this time the fourth plane return to the formation to symbolize that where the old ones fell, new ones are added.

When airbase Avno was closed in 1993, the Flying School moved to Karup. The small training aircrafts are still involved, but now they are coming all the way from Karup in Jutland to express the greeting and salute from the Danish Air Force to the fallen airmen buried at Svino by this special flying formation.

Until the closure of Airbase Avno it was also flying students from there, who were guardians at the graves through The May 4 ceremony. Now it is members of the Home Guard and soldiers associations who are guardians.

It is also members of the Home Guard, who are car park attendants, as a lot of people this evening will come to Svino.

In keeping with tradition the bagpipes orchestra 'Clan Rose Pipes and Drums of Denmark' is also participating.

Before the ceremony our gravedigger and church assistant through the last 40 years, Kirsten Andersen, has been very busy in cutting the grass and tidy the whole cemetery and the British graves as well, so that everything can look as nice as

possible the evening of May 4th.

Kirsten Andersen has through many years been nursing the graves of the airmen and in everything put great efforts in her work, so that the Memorial Grove always can look beautiful and be worth visiting.

Through the 27 years in which I now have been the vicar of Svino, there have often  been relatives to the airmen present at the commemoration, and sometimes during the day prior to the evening, interviews with the relatives have been arranged by newspapers and TV. When all the preparations have been completed, the day will come and the great May 4th event will take place.

It starts with a church service at 7.30pm in Svino church, which because of the subsequent flyover must not last longer than three quarters.

At 8,20pm the first flyover of the Air Force follows and at 8,23pm the next flyover takes place.

After the flyovers 'Clan Rose Pipes and Drums of Denmark' will be marching in to the Memorial Grove and there will be speeches, wreaths will be laid and music will be performed by the bagpipes orchestra.

Finally, I pray the Lord's Prayer and give the Benediction to the many participants and to the graves with the airmen, and we sing the hymn 'Always cheerful'.

The event is ending when a representative from the Guards Hussars is blowing 'Reveille' - not 'retreat' - as a symbol of resurrection.

Then the hundreds of people are leaving Svino again and surely returning on next May 4th.

After a cup of coffee in the village hall all the participants involved in the arrangement together with the invited guests driving the embassy cars with blue license plates and private chauffeurs are off again

And when the whole event is over and the guests have left, I always have to do an extra trip up in the Memorial Grove in the darkness. For at the monument 'Cross of Sacrifice' so many beautiful flowers and wreaths are laid as one can just make out in the darkness, and at all the British graves the candles flicker in the night and tell in more ways than one that 'The light shines in the darkness - and the darkness did not comprehend it! '.

Photos from May 4th 2003 by Joern Olav Ottosen – Above the Memorial Grove is seen with candles in the late evening

Improvement of Svino Memorial Grove

In 1990 Commonwealth War Graves Commission decided to put op information standards at all their cemeteries, so that visitors might be able to read about the cemetery, they visited.

Such a standard – in white stone with a stainless steel plate upon it with the engraving of historical details - was also placed at Svino Memorial Grove.

The standard has been made in weatherproof material, so that anyone – in Danish as

well as in English– can read the facts of the cemetery, they are visiting.

In 1994, Ron Wellings, an Englishman living in Denmark, had been visiting Svino Memorial Grove and found that it was a bit naked.

And perhaps it was.

Ron Wellings thought there was a lack of flowers.

He took the initiative and made the British Embassy donate an amount for the purchase of flowers to the memorial, and as the costs should not run up too much, it ended up that a representative from the embassy, some representatives from Svino Church council and Kirsten and Anders Bjornvad (author of Fallen Airmen), our gravedigger Kirsten Andersen and her husband and I met at Svino Memorial Grove on a Saturday in order to plant red roses and little blue plants, which had been bought for the donated amount

The colors were obviously chosen with care. Along with the white headstones the red roses and the little blue plants the colors symbolize the British nation, for which the young men, buried in the memorial grove, gave their lives.

Interment on May 4th, 1999
- Donald Smith and 7th Squadron Association

Visitors at Svino Memorial Grove may have noticed that in addition to the Cross of Sacrifice and all the British headstones and the monument for the in 1948-49 exhumed Americans, there is also a tombstone by design similar to the monument of the American airmen but slightly smaller.

This is the very last burial of an allied airman. However, he was not killed during the war but was actually the only survivor from a crash near Kirke Stillinge on April 21, 1943, where all his comrades were killed. He was flight engineer, but when he died in September 1998 he was ranked Major.

His name was Donald Smith and his tombstone, placed on the grave, is located respectfully 5 meters behind his fellow airmen, who died in the crash, and it says: "Together at last".

It was his great desire to be buried near his dead comrades from the War, despite the fact that he back in Canada had wife, as well as adult children and grandchildren.

But it was not that simple to fulfill his wish, as Svino Memorial Grove is now attached to Commonwealth War Graves Commission and is actually not open for burials.

Through the British Embassy I was told that the Commonwealth War Graves Commission could well allow the interment but would not permit that a tombstone was put up. If such was to be put up, it had to look quite different to the whites 'headstones', which were set up as tombstones of the allied airmen, who were killed during the war, and also there should be a minimum distance of 5 meters from this new burial site to the nearest graves from the war.

And it was done in that way.

Svino church council would also like to help mark the day, so it ended up that the interment took place on May 4, 1999 in the afternoon and started with coffee in Svino village hall.

Donald Smith's son is on the day of his father's interment putting flowers at the graves of his father's fellow airmen.
At Pilot Parish's grave, Parish's sister, Elizabeth Horsford, has placed a wreath.

The photo to the left shows Donald Smith's grave after the interment, but before the tombstone was put up.
At the top to the right three of Donald Smith's four sons are at their father's grave. At the bottom to the right the pilot Charles Parish's sister, Elizabeth Horsford (wearing a hat) is talking to (from the left) Jørgen Helme, Ron Wellings and Charles Lofthouse and his wife.

After the interment dinner was served in the vicarage in Kong to the approximately 50 involved people, and afterwards we celebrated May 4th in the evening at 7,30pm as usual.
The previous year a new bishop of Roskilde Diocese had been appointed, and before we had learned anything about Donald Smith's death and desire for interment at Svino cemetery, we had invited our new bishop, Jan Lindhardt, to conduct the May 4th service in 1999. He did not, however, attend the interment in the afternoon.
It was therefore a large dinner party, as many people did attend the interment.
Donald Smith's widow, Helen, did not manage to travel to Denmark, but three of their four sons with spouses came from Canada with Donald Smith urn.
In addition, representatives of the 7th Squadron's association (Donald Smith flew in the 7th sqd. during the war) attended the interment, as well as representatives from both the British and Canadian embassy, and Sylvia and Ejner Tjoern (former resistance fighters), who after the crash had helped Donald Smith to Sweden,. They themselves had to flee to Sweden the following year.

But actually I had met Donald Smith and his wife Helen before.
The couple had visited Denmark on several occasions since the war.
The first time was in 1968, when Helen Smith heard in Toronto Radio, Canada that a Dane was searching for her husband. The Dane was late Jorgen Helme, who has done a lot of work concerning investigation of crashed allied planes over Denmark during the war. He tried through the Canadian radio to find the Canadian survivor

from the crash near Kirke Stillinge on April 21, 1943.

In this way contact was established, and Donald Smith's first visit to Denmark was in 1968. At this tour he revisited several of the people, who had been hiding him and helping him to safety in neutral Sweden, as well as several of the places, where he had stayed on his route to Sweden.

In 1977 and in 1993 Donald Smith and his wife Helen visited Denmark again, and in 1993 I met them.

The reason for the visit in 1993 was that Farmer Helge Christiansen, Kirke Stillinge, 50 years after the crash had taken the initiative in erecting a memorial stone at the crash site in remembrance of the seven killed airmen from Donald Smiths's aircraft. As the only survival Donald Smith of course had to attend the unveiling of this memorial stone. Other members of the 7th SGD. Association attended the unveiling, too, as well as representatives from several embassies.

7th Squadron Association also visited Svino Memorial Grove, where I said a few prayers for them, and they placed flowers at the graves of Donald Smith's seven killed fellow airmen.

Donald Smith (nearest to the monument) and his wife Helen attending the prayers at Svino Memorial Grove when visiting in 1993

After his return to Canada Donald Smith wrote to me on July 5th 1993 saying:

" It was a very emotional time for me, but it was so nice to meet more of the Danish people and to see your beautiful country for the fourth time. The first time in 1943 wasn't that pleasant, but thanks to the brave members of the resistance and the farmers of Denmark, everything turned out OK."

None of us knew at the time that I would conduct his interment six years later. He might himself has had a clue, for later his son told that he already before the trip to Denmark was diagnosed with cancer, but because of the planned trip to Denmark together with 7 Squadron Association and the planned memorial unveiling, he chose to defer the initiation of treatment, until he was back in Canada again.

Donald Smith never drew any attention to his exploits in the war.

In fact he did not tell his children what had happened to him.

It was not until much later, they learned what their father had done during the war. That he miraculously was the first crashed allied airman who survived and got out of

Denmark to Sweden.

His son David Smith has later published his father's story on the Internet.

You can also read about Donald Smith's remarkable story in the little book: "First out of Denmark in 1943", written by Jorgen Nielsen and published by Albertslund Local History Society.

In addition, the journalist Peter Krüger made a TV broadcast in two parts on TV2 on Donald Smith.

Charles Lofthouse, who died 80 years old in 2002 and who during the war survived 37 bombing raids over Germany as well as 1½ year as POW (prisoner of war), was secretary in 7th Squadron Association and attended both the visit in 1993 as well as Donald Smith's interment in 1999. He wrote to me about Donald Smith in 1999:

Donald Smith, flight engineer in the Royal Canadian Air Force, flew with Charles Woodbine Parish and six others in the night on April 20, 1943 with Stettin as a target.

Charles Parish had just completed a series of operations with 149. Sqdrn. in Wellington planes from Mildenhall, 1940/41.

In 1942 he was placed in 75th Sqdrn. Newmarket and had to fly Sterling, now with a crew of three RAFVR (Royal Air Force Volunteer Reserve) and three RCAF (Royal Canadian Air Force) crew.

In January 1943, they chose Parthfinders and were recorded in the seventh Sqdrn. in Oakington.

They were eight that night on 20/21. April 1943. Wilfred Blake, RAF, also from Canada, who had recently come to the seventh Sqrdn. flew as a second pilot on this trip, which was to be a kind of 'introducing-trip' for him.

Early on the return flight one machine switched off due to serious oil leakage and loss of pressure.

Over Zealand they were attacked three times by a Messerschmitt 110, and despite heroic efforts they finally were given the order to jump.

Donald Smith was the only one of the crew members who managed to leave the machine and release his parachute.

Seven crew members died in the crash: Parish, Blake, Vance, Krulicki, Marshall, Farley and Lee. They were all buried at Svino.

Besætningen på Stirling I, R9261 (MG-M), der styrtede ned ved Kelstrup syd for Kirke Stillinge i de tidlige morgentimer d. 21. april 1943 efter et angreb af en tysk natjager. Stående fra venstre: R. Vance, D.V. Smith, C.W. Parish, J. Lees, og J.S. Marshall. Knælende: L. Krulicki og D.C. Farley. W.A. Blake, der mangler på billedet, var netop ankommet fra Canada og fulgte med som passager for at orientere sig om luftkrigen over Tyskland. Hele besætningen med undtagelse af D.V. Smith omkom og blev begravet på Svinø Kirkegård.

The above photo showing the crew of Donald Smith's aircraft was sent to me by Jorgen Helme in March 1999. It was Jorgen Helme, who made the contact to Donald Smith in 1968.

Donald Smith was the only one who succeeded in getting out of the plane, which crashed to the ground nose first after being attacked three times by the German night fighter. Donald Smith was sitting at the rear of the plane and used the bullet holes in the aircraft as handles, while he climbed upwards towards the tail of the plane and escaped in this way out of the falling aircraft. He landed in a plowed field, hid his parachute and then began to walk and run quickly to get as far away as possible from the crashed plane, so that the Germans would not find him.

He then walked for several days across Zealand from the field near Kirke Stillinge, where the plane had crashed, towards Copenhagen. On his way, he had several contacts with friendly Danes who helped hiding him and giving him food. It was by no means without danger - neither for the helping Danes nor for Donald Smith – as it was at that time of the war, when a cooperation between the Danish government and the German occupiers still existed. This meant that the Danes during this period were to report suspicious looking persons to the police, who then could arrest and surrender these people to the Germans. Donald Smith was therefore incredibly lucky with his contacts on his way.

In Herstedvester he came into contact with the resistance movement, who helped him to Elsinore. It turned out, however, that the ferry crossing was so well-guarded by the Germans that it was impossible to escape to Sweden. Donald Smith was again left alone and sought shelter in an empty holiday cottage but had a few days later again contact to the resistance movement. He was then questioned by Flemming B. Muus, who tried to have his identity confirmed by the intelligence service in London. He succeeded, and Donald Smith then spent a few days hiding at the homes of various resistance fighters in North Zealand, including Sylvia and Ejner Tjoern, who later attended his interment in 1999.

Donald Smith was then sent off in a canoe across the Sound together with another man and came - not without difficulties- to Sweden. Here he was initially detained as an illegal immigrant but came shortly after to Stockholm, where he and many others entered a plane to Scotland.

In Scotland, he again had to be questioned in order to establish his identity, before he - after a visit to the pilot Charles Parish's home - could travel back to Canada.

Donald Smith was the first allied airmen who succeed to escape from the occupied Denmark to Sweden.

A few words about the pilot of the aircraft, Charles Woodbine Parish:

Subsequently, I came into possession of a small book, authored by the father to Charles Woodbine Parish, the pilot of the aircraft. He writes very touchingly about his late son.

The father tells that Charles Parish was born in 1915 and grew up in a family of three brothers and a sister.

Their father took part in World War I.

In the years 1922-24, the family lived in Paris, where the father worked. The youngest child of the siblings, the sister Elizabeth (who visited her brother's grave in Svino memorial grove in both 1993 and 1999, where she attended Donald Smith's interment), was born in Paris.

Then the family moved back to England and had some happy years until the children lost their mother. Charles Parish was the eldest of the siblings and only 15, when their mother died.

Charles had an international education, with schooling at Eton, stays in India but also in southern Europe and in Germany, where he at first felt impressed by the emerging Nazism. He was educated in trade and office work but was in his spare time much interested in flying, and in 1939 he volunteered for service in the RAF, where he during the year went through an effective training.

In the period 1940-1943 he completed 54 bombing raids to Germany and Italy, and in September 1940 he survived as the only one from his plane a crash over the North Sea. He swam 11 km. during the night, while he oriented himself by the North Star. More dead than alive, he in the early morning reached the English coast.

After a period on land as a teacher and instructor, he again felt ready to fly, and again he took part in a series of bombing raids against Germany - until the fatal tour the night between April 20 and 21, 1943.

Having been attacked three times by a German night fighter, the aircraft was so damaged that Charles Parish had to give the crew his last order, as retold by Donald Smith in all its brief was:*"Sorry, boys, we'll have to jump."*

Charles Parish's father finishes his narrative of his son's life with the words:

"And so that morning, as parents at home prayed for their safety, this group of boys lay dead in and around their smouldering aircraft, having given all they had to give that others might live on in freedom.

So he passed over, and all the trumpets sounded for him on the other side."

After his death Charles Parish was awarded with the British decoration "Distinguished Flying Cross", and in "London Gazette" you could on November 5th, 1943 read about the decoration:

The King has approved the following award in recognition of gallantry and devotion to duty in the execution of air operations.

Distinguished Flying Cross

Flight Lieutenant Charles Woodbine Parish, Royal Air Force Volunteer Reserve, no. 7 Squadron (deceased) with effect from 14th March, 1943.

Flight Lieutenant Parish has attacked many targets in Germany and Italy. An exceptional pilot, he has always shown a calm precision in the face of heavy opposition. This officer, by his personal example, has contributed much to the high efficiency attained by his crew.

Charles Woodbine Parish, D.F.C. R.A.F. 1915-1943

More visits -

Through my now 27 years as a vicar of Kong and Svino I have received many visitors in Svino Memorial Grove - both groups, individuals, relatives, interested people and formal official visits as well. Obviously a lot of visitors have just visited the Memorial Grove without taking contact to neither vicar, gravedigger nor the prior of the church council.

In the following I will tell of some of the visits, which - in addition to the Donald Smith affair and the visit of no.7 Squadron Association both in 1993 and 1999 - has made a great impression on me.

The Cross family – relatives to P/O. Sydney Nelson Cross, RNZAF no.90 Squadron RAF

I started as a vicar of Kong and Svino in December 1989. To tell the truth I then did not know much of the Memorial Grove at Svino, but already on my first May 4th ceremony there were guests from afar. It was the brother of Sgt. John Wallace Henry, Ron Henry and his wife, and in addition the brother of P/O. Sydney Nelson Cross, Cliff Cross and his wife Paula.

Both couples, who otherwise did not know anything to each other, came from New Zealand's South Island – the Henry couple from Christchurch and the Cross-couple from a farm about 130 km south of Christchurch.

The Cross couple stayed during their visit with the now deceased chairman of the church council, Kurt Henriksen and his wife Jytte, who did not speak English, so much amusement came out of that fact.

For Cliff and Paula Cross it was their second visit to Denmark, as they a few years earlier had come unannounced to Denmark to visit Cliffs brother's grave.

At that time they came to Naestved railway station and took a taxi to Svino, where they came in contact with the chairman of the church council, Kurt Henriksen, who got hold of a young person who could speak English, and in that way they found out what the two New Zealanders wanted.

The visit in 1990 had been arranged in advance and was the beginning of a now more than 25-year long friendship between the Cross family in New Zealand and Kurt and Jytte Henriksen and family, their neighbors opposite, the brothers Joern and Leif Ottosen, and me and my son Gustav in the vicarage.

We decided that we would be their Danish family, and they would be our New Zealand family.

Since I learned to know Paula and Cliff Cross, the Cross family began to stay in the vicarage when they were visiting Svino, if not they were so many at a time that we had to put some of them up to the brothers Ottosen.

Members of the Cross family have visited Denmark many times - both on the occasion of May 4th ceremony and at other times of the year, if they have been to Europe.

For the family has other ties with Europe, too, as one grandson has found his wife in France, where the couple now resides, and also a new son-in-law has come from England, where the family also has several good friends.

Everybody in the family like to travel, and that means frequent visits at Nelson's grave.

Conversely, I have been to New Zealand visiting the Cross family several times during the last fifteen years.

This close relationship with a New Zealand family is a great enrichment and Karen (daughter of Cliff and Paula and niece of Sydney Nelson Cross buried at Svino Memorial Grove) has often said:

"Then Uncle Nelson did not die in vain!! His death has tied families together across the Earth. "

Paula and Cliff Cross died shortly after each other in 2011, but until her death, Paula every year sent greetings by mail with the wish for a lovely May 4th - if not they actually participated in the May 4th ceremony themselves.

When Paula and Cliff's daughter Karen in 2015 attended the May 4th ceremony at Svino, she was asked by a journalist, why she and her family continued to come to Svino and visit her uncle's grave - an uncle who after all had died long before, any of the remaining members of the Cross-family were born. The answer was really very simple. She said:

"But he is our flesh and blood!"

Sydney Nelson Cross died when he participated in the great overflying of Denmark on the night between April 20 and 21, where allied aircraft bombed Stettin and Rostock, and the RAF also lost about 20 aircrafts.

Sydney Nelson Cross was the pilot of a Stirling aircraft, who was to bomb Rostock. The plane, which had been attacked, crashed in the Great Belt near Korsor, and some of the bodies of the seven crew members were washed ashore between Korsor and Reersoe and others were recovered from the Great Belt.

Five of the airmen were buried in Svino cemetery and two at Bispebjerg Cemetery in Copenhagen.

Ron Henry – Brother of Sgt. John Wallace Henry, RNZAF no.9 Squadron RAF

At the same time as Paula and Cliff Cross visited Svino in the days around May 4, 1990, as mentioned, Ron Henry and his wife also visited Svino and participated in the May 4th celebration.

They stayed at Airbase Avno, and Lieutenant Colonel Thestrup hosted them.

Ron Henry's brother, Sgt. John Wallace Henry, was killed on September 24, 1942, when he participated in a bombing raid to Lubeck.

The plane, a Lancaster, was hit by shots and crashed on the way home near Hyllekrog on Lolland.

Only two of the seven crew members were found when their bodies drifted ashore on the coast.

John Wallace Henry was buried at Svino cemetery on October 22, 1942.

The second crew member, who was found, was Geoffrey William Ardern Higson, who was buried at Svino cemetery on October 9, 1942.

The remaining five crew members are supposed to have vanished in the sea.

Ron Henry brought with him a New Zealand flag, which Lieutenant Colonel Thestrup since the closure of Airbase Avno in 1993, has kept until recently, when he thought I should keep it in the vicarage.

Ron Henry had a kind of heroic poem composed to his brother, and he gave it to me for storage in the archive of the Memorial Grove.

The poem, which is very touching, is in many ways expressing the feelings of the relatives to the killed airmen.

The poem is shown on the photo below:

NZ 405266
SGT JOHN WALLACE HENRY ANZAC

SLUMBER ON THE VALIANT, SHED NOT YOUR UNWEPT TEAR,
HERO FROM A DISTANT PAST, YOU WHO KNEW NO FEAR.

SLEEP NOW YOU WELL, YOUR EARTHLY CLAY GROWN COLD,
TO REMAIN SO VERY YOUNG AS I GROW BENT AND OLD.

HANG NOT YOUR GINGER HEAD, HONOURED BROTHER MINE,
SON OF OUR LORD AND MASTER, THE GREAT ARCHITECT DIVINE.

EACH AND EVERY FOURTH OF MAY, TO THAT SACRIFICIAL CROSS,
TO HONOUR THOSE WHO LEFT US, LOVE'S LABOUR NEVER LOST.

FLOWERS PLACED O'ER YOUR HEAD IN CONSECRATED SOIL,
YOU ARE BUT THE WINNER OF SVINO'S LOVING TOIL.

WARRIORS AND VALKYRIES FROM VALHALLA'S HALLOWED HALL,
WILL ATTEND TO YOU IN VICTORY 'TIL ETERNITIES FINAL CALL.

I NOW DRAPE YOUR MEMORY WITH AN ENSIGN BLUE,
AS LONG AS DENMARK LIVES, YOU'LL ALWAYS BE ON VIEW.

WOULD I BUT TAKE YOU JACK, TO HALF A WORLD AWAY,
BUT YOUR EMBLEMS OF MORTALITY, IN SVINO WILL ALWAYS STAY.

FAREWELL TO YOU DEAR BROTHER, OUR MOTHER'S FAVOURITE SON,
WHO FOUGHT WITH HONOUR THEN CLIMBED INTO THE MORNING SUN.

TO YOU AND FELLOW KIWIS, I LEAVE WHILE YOU REMAIN,
'TIL ERE WE MEET ONCE MORE AND JUST BE BOYS AGAIN.

COMPOSED BY JOCK TURNER FOR RONALD HENRY
FOR THE 4TH MAY 1990

Betty Willis – the widow of P/O George Harold Willis RAF no. 158. Squadron

In late August 1993, I received a letter from Port Alfred, South Africa.
The letter was from Betty Willis, who along with her sister would come to Denmark in September to visit her husband's grave on Svino cemetery.
She had got my name, address and telephone number through the Danish consulate in Johannesburg and told me the place and time of her arrival and also where she would reside in Copenhagen and Naestved in the days she was in Denmark.
It was important for her to visit her husband's grave that year, as it was 50 years since he died.
She wrote that she had also visited the grave in 1980, but since it was winter at that time and everything was covered in snow, and it was her impression that the church was no longer in use, she therefore looked forward to seeing the grave properly this time, as she because of the snow in 1980 had not seen the grave since she attended the opening of Svino Memorial Grove in 1950.
As a matter of fact Svino Church was in use in 1980, but I can imagine that the heavy snow has made Svino appear as a remote, desolate area.
The day came when I met Betty Willis at Svino cemetery.
She told me that she and 'Hal', as she called her husband George Harold Willis, only had been married for nine months when he died, and that they had only been together the first three months, because he during the last six months of their marriage had participated in the war and flown for the RAF.
She had never remarried.
It was the third time she visited her husband's grave.
"This will probably be my last visit," she said, for she was by that time an old lady, and there is a long way from Port Alfred in South Africa to Svino.
She had brought photos of George Harold Willis and flowers - both for the grave and for the altar in Svino church, where she sat in to be alone and think back.
George Harold Willis died when he attended a great overflight of Denmark on the night between April 20 and 21, 1943.
The aircrafts were on a bombing raid to Stettin and Rostock.
George Harold Willis' plane, a Halifax from RAF 158th Squadron, was to bomb Stettin but was hit by the Germans and crashed at Drosselbjerg Cliff.
Three aircrafts were shot down over Zealand that night, and all the dead crew members - except for two, who were buried in Bispebjerg Cemetery in Copenhagen - were taken to Svino to be buried there.
But actually Colonel Helge Gram told me in a letter of Oct. 31, 1994, that the RAF lost 20 aircrafts of Denmark that night together with 144 crew members. The 115 of them died. 80 were buried identified. 20 vanished in ocean and sounds. 15 have so far been buried unidentified. 28 became prisoners of war. Only one succeeded in escaping to Sweden (and it was previously mentioned Donald Smith). The letter from Colonel Gram was also about an identification problem, he had just solved concerning an unidentified airman buried in Esbjerg, who now could be identified.
Maybe it was because there were so many dead persons at one time or perhaps it was for completely different reasons that the Germans, when they brought the dead airmen in coffins to Svino, erroneously reported that in the coffin, which was buried in grave no. 9, was an unknown airman whose characteristic was a ring with the initials BMW and a shoulder strap reading "Rhodesia".

After Betty Willis' visit, I have been wondering why her husband and she was listed as being from Chelsea, England, when looking up George Harold Willis in the Commonwealth War Graves records, which are available on the Internet, as I could see that according to the church records, a non-identified airman had been buried in grave no. 9 wearing a ring with the initials BMW and a shoulder strap reading Rhodesia - However, in April 1946 rightfully identified as buried in grave no. 24 - see. p.24.

The crash place and date corresponded with George Harold Willis, so I did not understand why his wife was said to be from Chelsea in England, now that I knew - both from church records and from his wife that they rightfully were from Rhodesia, now Zimbabwe.

A closer examination of the archive of Svino Memorial Grove, however, could help explain this.

Here I came across a letter from Betty Willis to Reverend Lindelov dated February 24, 1946, Cape Town, South Africa. At this time she had not yet been told where her husband was buried, nor whether he actually had died and been buried. She had just been told that he was missing and that several other crew members from his plane were buried at Svino.

In the letter, she naturally expressed the hope that her husband was still alive and perhaps roaming about somewhere in Europe, but at the same time she asks Reverend Lindelov whether there could be any possibility that an airman was buried at Svino, who wore a ring with the inscription BMW, which was her initials and the date 27-7-42, which was the day they were married.

At this time, her husband had been buried for almost three years at Svino, and two months later in April 1946 he was identified by the Missing Research Enquiry in grave no. 24, where he was lying wearing his wedding ring with his wife's initials and date of their wedding engraved in the ring.

The poor woman had for three years only known, he was reported missing. She had obviously feared the worst, with good reason, it turned out. Now she, however, was assured that her husband had died and where he was buried.

Four years later, she participated in the opening of Svino Memorial Grove.

There is even a letter from her sent some days after the opening of the memorial grove May 5, 1950, where she is writing to thank Reverend Lindelov for the beautiful ceremony, and because she and another widow had stayed overnight in the rectory.

In this letter, sent from Chelsea in England, she writes that she the day after her arrival back again was at the office, which of course indicates that Betty Willis in a period had lived and worked in Chelsea. This is probably the reason, why CWGC about George Harold Willis has recorded that he was married to Betty Willis from Chelsea.

This, despite the fact that Betty Willis both in 1945 wrote from South Africa and in 1993 traveled to Svino from her home in Port Alfred, South Africa, and although her husband George Harold Willis rightfully was one of the many volunteers from Rhodesia, who volunteered for service in the RAF during the war.

Colin Fowler – a survived airman from RNZAF no.75 Squadron

The year after, Donald Smith in 1993 together with the 7th Squadron Association had visited Svino Memorial Grove, another survivor of a plane crash was visiting Svino. Also his fellow crewmembers had been buried at Svino cemetery.

50 years after his crash Colin Fowler would like to pay his dead comrades a visit. Colin Fowler was only 19 years old, when he on September 12, 1944 crashed in a Lancaster aircraft from Squadron 75, along with William James Victor Boyd, John Patrick Arthur Giles, John Bernard Gudgeon, John Matthew Biggar, Wilson Orchard Hadley and Jack Wilcox.

The plane caught fire during a mine laying operation and crashed into a house near Orslev, north of Vordingborg, where the family Pommergaard lived.

When the plane hit the property, the couple Pommergaard and three adult children were killed.

At the same time five of the seven crew members on the plane were killed.

It was a terrible tragic accident with a total of 10 fatalities. Only Colin Fowler and Jack Wilcox survived by parachuting.

Boyd, Giles and Gudgeon were buried the following day, September 13, 1944, at Svino cemetery. But when they cleaned up at the crash site, they also found the bodies of Biggar and Hadley. These were by the Germans ordered to be buried by the gravedigger at Orslev Cemetery without any ceremony, but the vicar of Orslev, Mr. Hoyer-Christensen, conducted the gravesite ceremony on Sunday Sept. 24, 1944 after his regular church service.

The five deaths from the family Pommergaard were buried immediately next to the two airmen at Orslev cemetery.

One survivor, Jack Wilcox, was captured by the Germans and spent the rest of the war in a German prisoner of war camp, until he after the war was able to return to his home in New Zealand.

Colin Fowler sought initially to hide in Orslev Church, and later he with help from friendly Danes reached Copenhagen and came to Sweden.

During his visit to Denmark in 1994 Colin Fowler participated with his son Neil at a service in Svino Church and visited his fellow airmen's graves at Svino Memorial Grove. Later in the day, he attended a church service in Orslev Church.

The son took up both worships on video, so that Fowler subsequently could send a copy to Wilcox, who lived in New Zealand and could not attend the 50 years celebration – due to both distance and his advanced age. Moreover, Colin Fowler could also show the video to his wife, as she was forced to stay in England, because she suffered so badly from asthma that she was not able travel abroad.

Colin Fowler said that throughout his life he had continued to ponder why his own and Wilcox's life were saved in the crash, when at the same time ten other people died.

After his return to England Colin Fowler wrote in a letter to me about the visit:

"As you will no doubt understand, it was an emotional time for me, and looking back as I stood at the gravesides, it hardly seemed possible that 50 years have passed, since my fellow airmen and friends died, and also the great tragedy suffered by the Pommergaard family……In the afternoon a similar event took place at Orslev Church, where I was able to pay my respects, not only to the other crew members, but also to the 5 Pommergaard family.

This particular church has many memories for me, for it was within the church walls, I took refuge after I had landed by parachute, and I had some 5-6 hours to think about what had occurred and wonder, what was going to happen, before help arrived in the morning."

Veterans from Montgomery's 8th Army -

In the summer of 1995 we had a visit in the Memorial Grove, which was a little special.

A Danish veteran club for soldiers had connection to veterans of Montgomery's 8th Army - also called "The desert Rats" - and invited them to visit in Denmark.

On the day of their visit, July 7, they had been guests at a lunch at the barracks of the hussars, at that time located in Naestved, and in the early afternoon a group of festive elderly gentlemen arrived to Svino church in the company of their Danish friends.

Since a few of them were from Scotland, both kilt and nice tartan trousers were represented amongst the clothing, which also included jackets with all the many medals they had received and berets in different designs. They also brought a tab.

I had prepared a service for them totaly in English. Still, I was not quite prepared for their behavior, as they behaved as you usually do at services in England: They sat down during Bible readings and stood up during the hymns. In Denmark we do just the opposite.

After the service we held a small ceremony outside in the Memorial Grove, where they laid a wreath at the Cross of Sacrifice.

Veterans from Montgomery's 8th Army – The dessert Rats – visiting Svino on July 7th, 1995

73

Later in the afternoon I followed them back to the barracks of the hussars in order to tour the stables and the fine museum at the barracks, and the day ended with a barbecue event in the target range, where they both sang and told stories, and for one reason or another they found it very amusing that both Colonel Guldberg's wife and I had to try on their Scottish berets.

It was a very pleasant day, and it's hard to understand that these festive elderly gentlemen once had been the tough 'desert rats' who in the war fought under extremely difficult and demanding conditions in North Africa. Indeed, it is said that it was the battle of El-Alamein, which was one of the turning points in the 2nd World War, as Field Marshal Montgomery's 8th Army here had pushed the Germans out of Egypt. This turning point in the war was actually due to these pleasant elderly men!

Phil Goff, Minister of Foreign Affairs and Trade of New Zealand

An afternoon in late summer 2002, the phone rang in the vicarage, and when I took it, a male voice in English reported that he was calling from the New Zealand Embassy in Brussels on behalf of Ambassador Dell Higgie. (New Zealand has no embassy in Denmark; therefore matters relating to Denmark are taken care of during the embassy in Brussels.)

His intention was that the New Zealand Trade and Foreign Minister, Phil Goff, would come to Copenhagen from 19th-20th September to participate in the negotiations between New Zealand and the EU, but when he was in Denmark, the ambassador wanted to fit in a little different element to his program.

It had also become aware that a New Zealand Minister had never visited the Commonwealth War Graves in Denmark. Mr. Goff would therefore like to be the first minister to do this, in order to commemorate the New Zealand airmen who died in Danish territory during World War II. Therefore, the question from the embassy secretary was, if I could receive their Trade -and Foreign Minister Phil Goff, at Svino Memorial Grove on the afternoon September 19.

"Well, I could surely do that", I stammered surprised, and then it struck me that a guest coming from so far away had to be offered something, so I asked, if I then was allowed to invite the Minister for afternoon coffee - or tea (New Zealand is a tea-drinking race with deep British traditions!).

"Well, maybe," was the reply, "but he had to find out, if it was possible, as the minister had a rather busy schedule".

And so it happened that New Zealand's trade and Foreign Minister Phil Goff an afternoon in September 2002, arrived to Svino Memorial Grove in a – for the occasion - lent Danish ministerial car with a police escort.

Anders Bjornvad (who has made an incredible work to find out and write about the historical data on the allied airmen crashed and buried in Denmark) and his wife Kirsten had also been involved in the visit, and together with our gravedigger and church assistant Kirsten Andersen and chairman of the church council Kurt Henriksen we were waiting at the entrance to Svino cemetery to greet the minister. In the Memorial Grove, I conducted a short English worship after which the Minister laid a wreath at the Cross of Sacrifice.

When the police escort saw, how peaceful everything was at Svino, they went away again, and after the visit to the Memorial Grove, where Phil Goff interested looked at

74

the many graves, we went to the vicarage and had afternoon coffee - and tea! in my dining room, while my son, who at that time was 10 years old, tried to sit in the ministerial car.

In the company was also Ambassador Dell Higgie together with the embassy secretary, who a month earlier had phoned me regarding the visit.

Phil Goff, Minister of Foreign Affairs and Trade of New Zealand visiting the vicarage.

The visit to the vicarage lasted for about an hour before the busy minister had to go back to Copenhagen.

But it was a wonderful and exciting day for all of us.

The last time I saw Phil Goff, however, was when I met him shortly in New Zealand four months later, when I was visiting the Cross family (relatives of one of the airmen buried in Svino).

I was in the capital Wellington for a few days, and participated in a guided tour of the government building.

Before the tour started, I went to the information desk in order to ask, if Phil Goff was in the house that day, as it would be nice to say hello again. So I introduced myself and was told that he actually was in the house, and that he would like to meet me and my son, but it would be quite short, as he was busy with meetings and negotiations throughout the day.

We just had to follow our guided tour of the house, and we would then be picked up and taken to Phil Goff's office, when he had a break between meetings.

And suddenly in the middle of our tour of the government building, we were picked up by two security guards and escorted to an elevator and taken up to Phil Goff's front office, where we waited for a moment before he came rushing in with an entourage of suit-dressed secretaries and other accompanying staff. It was a little short meeting where we talked about graves of allied airman, Denmark and holiday in New Zealand, and then he was on to the next meeting, and we were led back to the ongoing tour of the government building.

The ambassador, who visited on bike -

It happened far more informal, when the US ambassador to Denmark, James P. Cain, had decided to tour Denmark by stages on bike, before his term of office in the country ended.

During his route through the municipality of Vordingborg, it was decided that he should pay Svino Memorial Grove a visit.

The then Mayor Henrik Holmer, had decided to cycle with the ambassador through the municipality of Vordingborg and met with him in the middle of the bridge to Falster, and Mr. Karsten Nonbo who was to follow the ambassador through the municipality of Naestved, was also in the group of cyclists as they one day late in August 2007 turned the corner to Svino church road and came towards the cemetery.

The head of the church council, Kurt Henriksen, and gravedigger and church assistant, Kirsten Andersen, and I met them, and present were also a few representatives from the local historical archives. They took some photos from the visit to the archive, while I showed the ambassador around in the memorial grove and told about the background to it - and not least, told him of the American airmen who had also been buried here but had been exhumed in 1948-49.

It was a cozy and informal short meeting with an ambassador, who really wanted to learn to know the country, in which he for four years was US ambassador.

The ride also caused interest and respect among the Danes, and both in TV and newspapers we could follow how far the US ambassador had come on his route through our small country.

Ambassador James P. Cain in Svino Memorial Grove on his knees in front of the memorial stone for the American airmen, who were buried here until 1948-49, while I'm telling him about the Memorial Grove.
The then Mayor Henrik Holmer is watching from behind the Ambassador and gravedigger and church assistant, Kirsten Andersen, is only just to be seen to the left side.

Jenny Weintroub – niece to Sgt. Maurice Gruber RAF no. 50. Squadron

In the summer of 2008, I got an email from Jenny Weintraub.
She and her husband and some friends were on a tour in Scandinavia, and as she was the niece of Sgt. Maurice Gruber, who was buried at Svino, she would therefore like to pay a visit to her uncle's grave.
She came from South Africa, and no one in her family had, as far as she knew, ever visited her uncle's grave.
I met them in Svino Memorial Grove and had made a pot of coffee with something to eat as well, packed into a basket. We sat on the bench near the church and talked a little, after they had visited the grave.
Jenny Weintroubs uncle, Maurice Gruber was from Rhodesia, the present Zimbabwe.
He had - as many of his fellow countrymen as well - signed up as a volunteer for service in the RAF, and so had his brother Rufus Isaacs Gruber, who was also killed and is now buried in a Commonwealth cemetery in Hamburg, Germany.
Their parents were left in Mashaba in Southern Rhodesia having lost two sons in the war.
Maurice Gruber was 30 years old, when he died. It was on a bombing raid to Warnemünde on May 9, 1942. He was the pilot on a Manchester aircraft, which had been hit by the Germans and crashed on Moen at St. Linde near Damsholte.
Maurice Gruber was the only crew member who died in the crash.
The other six crew members were taken prisoner by the Germans.
Maurice Gruber was the first allied airman, who was buried at Svino.
The funeral was conducted by a German chaplain from Copenhagen and was a spectacular - but of course German - military funeral, where the German military shot honorary salute over his grave.
Maurice Gruber was of Jewish origin, and his tombstone is the only one of the Allied headstones adorned with the Star of David.
Jenny Weintroub and her husband laid flowers at the grave, and took photos of each other at the headstone of a family member buried so many thousands of kilometers away from his - and their - homeland.

Max Abbott – brother to Sgt. Clifford Abbott, RAF no.75 Squadron

In the archive of Svino Memorial Grove, there is a letter from Ernest Abbott. His son Sgt. Clifford Abbott RAF no.75 Squadron is buried at Svino.
The letter is dated July 16, 1950 and addressed to Reverend Lindelov and the purpose of the letter is thanking Reverend Lindelov. Ernest Abbott and his wife had attended the impressive opening of Svino Memorial Grove and at the same time visited the grave of their son Clifford.
In the letter the father also tells about his son Clifford, how he volunteered for the RAF and how he grew up in the countryside and was very fond of the nature, and that the rural and remote Svino cemetery close to nature, therefore is a very appropriate place for his son's grave.
Ernest Clifford says that he and his 20-year-old daughter might come later that year and visit the grave. He had hoped that the younger son could have come with them, he writes, but the son had to stay home and care for his school. If father and daughter

came to Denmark and visited Clifford's grave that year is not known, but it took 59 years before the youngest son Max visited Svino Memorial Grove.

Dear Madam,

On 5th May this year we in Denmark are commemorating the fifth anniversary of the liberation of our country from the Germans by Field Marshal Montgomery's armies.

During the long years of occupation our hope of liberation was based on the victories of the Allied armies, and it will never be forgotten in Denmark that it is very much due to their great efforts, and not least to the Royal Air Force, that our country can celebrate her independence and her existence as one of the free nations of the world.

We can never repay our debt to those splendid men, but as a small token of gratitude, the Danish Government has decided to invite two relatives each of British Service Men, buried in Denmark, to visit our country in connection with the anniversary of the liberation.

On behalf of the people of Denmark I am, therefore, glad to extend an invitation to you to come to Denmark as the guests of the Danish Government. The invitation covers your journey and stay in Denmark. If you are able to accept this invitation I shall arrange for the necessary details about your journey and your stay in Denmark to be sent to you.

Will you be good enough to address your reply to the Danish Ambassador, 29, Pont Street, London, S.W.1.

Yours sincerely,

PRIME MINISTER OF DENMARK

In May 2009, Clifford Abbott's younger brother Max and his wife Gwen from North Yorkshire in England came to visit. They would like to participate in the May 4th ceremony in Svino Church and Memorial Grove and also visit the grave of Max's brother Clifford and the graves of his fellow airmen as well. The years had passed and Max had not previously visited his brother's grave. Of course, he had seen photos and his father and mother had told him about their visit at the opening of the Memorial Grove in 1950, but it was something else being there himself, he said. Max Abbott handed me a copy of a letter, the Danish government in 1950 sent out to relatives of the allied military personnel who were killed during the war and were buried in Danish cemeteries.

In the letter, signed by then Prime Minister Hans Hedtoft, two relatives per killed allied soldier were invited to come to Denmark and participate in the celebration of Liberation Day in 1950 - five years after the liberation.

The invitation would cover both travel and stay in Denmark, it was told.

The fifth anniversary of the liberation would be celebrated at several places in Denmark, especially at all the cemeteries where allied soldiers had been buried during the war.

This invitation was therefore accepted by many relatives – including the parents of Clifford Abbott.

After the visit in 2009 Max Abbott wrote in a letter to me:

"The commemoration service was very impressive and at times very emotional. We have a video recording of your complete church service and highlights of the ceremony before the Cross of Sacrifice. We are so contented that the Danish people are looking after my dear brother Clifford, members of his crew and fellow airmen, in such a wonderful way. It was heartbreaking to lose my brother in 1943 and we think of him every day and although he was a volunteer and did not need to be in the armed service, we have to believe that he did not die in vain."

Max Abbott gave to me this copy of a photo of his brother Clifford and his fellow crew members.

Clifford Abbott's aircraft, a Stirling from RAAF no.75 Squadron, took part in a mine-laying operation done by the RAF on the night between April 28 and 29, 1943 over the Baltic Sea and several smaller Danish waters.

During the operation at least 10 RAF aircrafts crashed this night over Danish territory.

Clifford Abbott's plane was to throw down mines over Kiel bay.

The entire crew of seven perished and were all buried at Svino.

The crew consisted of three Britons, Sgt. Clifford Abbott, RAF, Sgt. John Thomas Glendinning, RAF, Sgt. George Phillips, RAF, two New Zealanders, P/O. Desmond Lewis Thomson, RNZAF, Wt. / O. Ernest Jenkins, RNZAF, an Australian, F/Sgt. John Muir Williams, RAAF and a Canadian, Wt. /O. James Alexander Ramsay, RCAF.

Rosalind Elliott – daughter of F/Lt. Wilfred John Parsons RAF no.158 Squadron

Rosalind and Ted Elliott attended the May 4th ceremony in 2013.

They came in the company of Ron Wellings, an English gentleman living in Denmark, who for many years now has been a very kind and helpful intermediary and facilitator of contacts to the relatives of the allied airmen.

Rosalind Elliott is the daughter of F/Lt. Wilfred John Parsons from no.158 Squadron. He was killed when his plane took part in the bombing raid to Stettin on the night between April 20 and 21, 1943.

He actually also was in the same aircraft as previously mentioned P / O. George Harold Willis from Rhodesia.

The aircraft was attacked by the Germans and crashed into the sea off Drosselbjerg Cliff on the night, when RAF - according to information in the letter from Colonel Helge Gram - lost 20 aircrafts over Danish territory.

Rosalind Elliott was just one year old, when her father died.

On the list of attendances at the opening of Svino Memorial Grove, one can see that it was her father's sister with her husband, who on behalf of the family attended the ceremony. I'm not aware, if her mother, F/Lt. Parsons' wife, has ever seen his grave.

Now, however, Parsons' daughter came on the 70th anniversary of his death and visited the grave together with her husband and took part in the commemoration of May 4th.

She was fascinated by the fact that so many people attended the commemoration and wanted to somehow show her gratitude to the Danes, and it resulted in a very nice small gift with a special history.

RAF no. 158 Squadron had their base at the airfield of Lisset, near Bridlington in East Yorkshire.

A few years ago, the artist Peter Wallwork Naylor made a more than two meter high sculpture in sheet metal by a seven-man crew from no. 158 Squadron in remembrance of all those who served in no.158 Squadron during World War II and especially in memory of the 851 crew members who perished in the bombing raids over Germany.

Rosalind Elliott therefore asked the artist to make two miniature versions of this great sculpture and sent both replicas to Ron Wellings and asked him to distribute them.
Ron Wellings immediately sent one sculpture for me to set up in Svino Church, and now this small and very expressive sculpture is placed above the door from the church to the porch, so that no one can leave Svino church without a glance at this beautiful little sculpture and send a thought back to the World War II and to all the airmen who gave their lives fighting for our freedom.
As Rosalind Elliot in an accompanying letter, wrote:

"I appreciate that this replica commemorates the 158 Squadron but I would like to think that it represents all the fliers who lost their lives and are buried in Svino churchyard."

Miniature version of the monument to RAF no.158. Squadron, at Lisset Airfield made by Peter Wallwork Naylor

A group of people connected with Svino Memorial Grove -

Among my personal papers, letters and matters of Svino Memorial Grove, I found this photo, which I've received from Bob Cobley while he was employed at the British Embassy.

The photo is not dated, but I think it's from one of the years just around the millennium.

It was taken at a garden party at the British ambassador's residence, "Bernstorffshoj" in Gentofte on the occasion of HM Queen Elizabeth's birthday.

I found the photo interesting, because the persons on the photo in different ways all are connected with Svino Memorial Grove and its history over the past 30-50 years.

At the very edge to the left the longstanding and colorful chairman of Svino Church Council, the late Kurt Henriksen is standing.

Kurt Henriksen, who died in 2012, was the son of Farmer Georg Henriksen, who was churchwarden at Svino during the war. Kurt Henriksen therefore grew up with the graves of the allied airmen at Svino cemetery and the events concerning the funerals of the more than 100 allied airmen close in on him. These experiences have rooted themselves in him and developed to that love and affection, he felt throughout his life towards the buried airmen and the many relatives who over the years have come to visit their dead family members.

But Kurt Henriksen was also a committed and enthusiastic storyteller about Svino Memorial Grove for the many, many visitors, groups as well as individuals, who through the years have come to see the allied graves at Svino, and he could certainly have added more stories to the history of Svino Memorial Grove than I've been able to tell in this little book.

Next to Kurt Henriksen is now deceased Kirsten Bjornvad standing in a dark dress with a flower on it. Kirsten was married to Anders Bjornvad, who is on the far right of the photo and was an invaluable support to him in his great work on the investigation of the allied airmen buried in Denmark during the war.
He could as a joke refer to her as "his unpaid secretary".

Next to Kirsten Bjornvad is now deceased Chamberlain, Colonel Helge Gram and (closest to Kirsten Bjornvad) his wife lic.phil. Gerda Gram.
When Helge Gram retired from the Armed Forces, he worked tirelessly in trying to identify the allied airmen who during the war had been buried as unknown around at the Danish cemeteries. He actually succeeded in solving some of the identification tasks.
Throughout the last half of the 1990s, I had a fairly close correspondence with Helge Gram, who in this period just started to work on the identification of the eight airmen buried as unknown at Svino cemetery during the war.
But unfortunately Helge Gram did not succeed to identify any of the on Svino cemetery buried airmen.
Helge Gram has also written the very interesting and informatively book "Shot down over Denmark 1940-1945"

Next to Helge Gram I'm standing, now for 27 years a vicar of Kong and Svino. The contact to the many relatives, visitors and interested in Svino Memorial Grove has enriched my life to such an extent that I am deeply grateful to all what "my" dead airmen posthumously have taught me about life understanding, wisdom, and not least: the love of a cause and to a country.

Just behind me is Bob Cobley - or more correct: now former Senior Commercial Officer Robert Graham Cobley, MBE (Most Excelent Order of the British Empire) - who more than anyone in relation to Svino Memorial Grove has been the personification of the British Embassy to us here in South Zealand.
Bob Cobley has participated in numerous May 4th celebrations in Svino both private and as a representative of the British Embassy. We have planted roses and blue flowers at the Memorial Grove together, and he has in many ways been a key intermediary in relation to the embassy, British conditions and the Commonwealth War Graves Commission.
Bob Cobley has now retired from working at the British Embassy and is now Honorary Representative of Denmark, Commonwealth War Graves Commission.

Next to me is gravedigger and church assistant Kirsten Andersen, who for nearly 40 years has taken care of not only Svinø church and cemetery but also Svinø Memorial Grove.
She has an agreement with the Commonwealth War Graves Commission of attending The Memorial Grove, in parallel with her employment by the Church Council to take care of the cemetery and the church.
You have to look long for a more conscientious and committed gravedigger.
Kirsten Andersen have put blood, sweat and tears in the care of the Memorial Grove

and engaged not only her late husband Niels, but also her three daughters and their husbands and children in the work.

At the time of writing, Kirsten Andersen is beginning partially to retire from work, as she is now 70 years old, but she'll continue living close to the Memorial Grove, so she can keep an eye on everything and see if it's looking tidy.

And I'm sure she will do so!

Next to Kirsten Andersen on the far right of the photo is now deceased Anders Bjornvad.

Anders Bjornvad was in 1990 decorated with the British order: The Most Excellent Order of the British Empire. And the award was well deserved!

Anders Bjornvad has since 1970 worked hard to identify, search for, collect and record historical accounts of the allied airmen who crashed over Danish territory during World War II. It resulted in the thorough and carefully prepared book "Fallen airmen 1939-1945" but also "They found a way" which is a book about the surviving airmen and their escape out of Denmark. Finally, he has written his memoirs: "A handshake in a crosswalk."

Both Anders and Kirsten Bjornvad helped to plant red roses and blue flowers at Svino Memorial Grove, as well as they participated in the visit of New Zealand's Trade and Foreign Minister Phil Goff. Moreover, they at many occasions visited Svino Memorial Grove together with guests and relatives of the airmen.

I'm uncertain who the gentleman standing immediately behind Anders Bjornvad is, but I think it might be the former Canadian ambassador who participated in Donald Smith's interment on May 4 1999.

Unfortunately I have to write 'deceased' or 'late' about several of the people with relations of one kind or another to Svino Memorial Grove, who appear on the photo from the ambassador's residence, 'Bernstorffshoj'. I therefore thought that it might be time to write this small book, before we are all dead, and no living person will remember the visits of the relatives and their stories and memories of their dead family members, the allied airmen, who gave the most precious thing they could give in the struggle for our freedom and now lie buried in Svino Memorial Grove - far from their own and their family's homeland.

The buried
– Summary of allied airmen, buried at Svino Memorial Grove

Below you will find a summary of the allied airmen, buried at Svino.
I have decided to gather the airmen, who flew in the same plane, and give a brief introduction regarding the aircraft - which task it had, and where and when it crashed.
For each person there is a photo of his headstone, and his rank and full name. Origin and age is shown if possible.
I also tell where and when he is found, and when he is buried.
If an inscription is found on the headstone it is reported, too.

Grave Numbers

In the upcoming review of the buried, you might be a little confused regarding the grave numbers, since they are not continuous processed. This is due to several factors.
For one thing, the 26 first buried airmen were exhumed and reburied in the Memorial Grove after the war, where some airmen at that time already had been buried, since the new part of the cemetery became operational at the beginning of the 1944.
For another, the two first buried airmen (who initially were buried in the middle of the existing cemetery at Svino) subsequently received grave numbers denoted by Roman numerals I and II.
In addition, the next buried were not buried right next to each other. Therefore for example, grave no. 5a and 5b are earlier than grave no. 1.
It may also confuse that the crash and thus time of death is not necessarily immediately before the funeral date (and thus the allocation of grave number), since in some cases long time passed before a perished airman was found.
An extra confusion regarding the grave numbers is the fact that the grave numbers might be assigned sequentially in proportion to the time of the burial, but the American grave numbers don't exist anymore. Nevertheless there hasn't been any change in the remaining British grave numbers.
Therefore, it may also wonder a little that we still operate with grave numbers up to no. 97, although of course, after the Americans were exhumed and moved, we only have the 62 British graves left.

Date for the gravesite ceremony:

I have written the date for the gravesite ceremony for those airmen, who were buried during 1944, as the airmen from the spring of 1944 on the German command simply were buried at the cemetery without any funeral service, but at the first service in Svino Church after new graves were added, prayers and gravesite ceremony were conducted at the new graves - despite the German ban. This practice began, however, in reality, already in late autumn 1943, but in the last months of 1943, only Americans were buried who have since been exhumed. Therefore they are not included in the following, where I have chosen to focus on the remaining 62 British airmen.

A Manchester aircraft (bomber), no. 50 Sqadron crashed on May 9, 1942 at St. Linde near Damsholte, Moen.

The aircraft took part in a bombing raid to Warnemünde and was hit by the Germans. On board the plane were seven crew members. Gruber, who was the pilot, was the only one who died. The other six crew members were taken prisoner by the Germans.

Sgt. Maurice Gruber, RAF
(Volunteer, Southern Rhodesia).
Age 30.
Buried May 13, 1942.
Grave I.
Inscription:
In everloving memory of our dear son.
Deeply mourned by parents, sister and
brothers

A Wellington aircraft (mine laying) of the 9th Squadron crashed on May 16, 1942 in Nakskov Fjord, Lolland.

The aircraft took part in a mine-laying operation in the southern Great Belt but was hit by the Germans and crashed into the sea off Nakskov.

The aircraft's radio operator was killed in the crash, while four of the aircraft's crew members were rescued by the police to Nakskov hospital. Two other crew members are supposed to have disappeared in the sea.

Sgt. (wireless operator/air gunner)
Albert Grouchy, RAF (volunteer, St.
John's Newfoundland).
Age 20.
Buried May 20, 1942.
Grave II.
Inscription:
Grant him eternal rest, o Lord, and
light perpetual to shine upon him

A Lancaster aircraft (bomber) of the 9th Squadron crashed on September 23, 1942 in the Baltic Sea.
The plane exploded in the air on the way home from a bombing raid.
The crew - except for two that were buried in Svino - disappeared in the sea

Sgt. James William Carnley, RAAF
(New South Wales, Australia).
Age 23.
Found near Hyllekrog, Lolland on September 24, 1942.
Buried October 9, 1942.
Grave 5a.
Inscription:
His duty nobly done

Sgt. Charles Francis Watson, RAAF
(New South Wales, Australia).
Age 22.
Found near Nysted, Lolland on September 26, 1942.
Buried October 9, 1942.
Grave 5b.
Inscription:
He heard his country call, he willingly gave his all. We cannot forget.

A Lancaster aircraft (bomber) of the 9th Squadron crashed on September 24, 1942 near Hyllekrog, Lolland.
The plane crashed on bombing raid to Lubeck.
All perished. Five crew members disappeared in the sea. Two were buried in Svino.

Sgt. (flight engineer) Geoffrey William Higson, RAF (volunteer, Manchester, England)
Age 28.
Washed ashore and found near Holsteinborg on September 28, 1942
Buried October 9, 1942.
Grave 3.
Inscription:
Rembrance

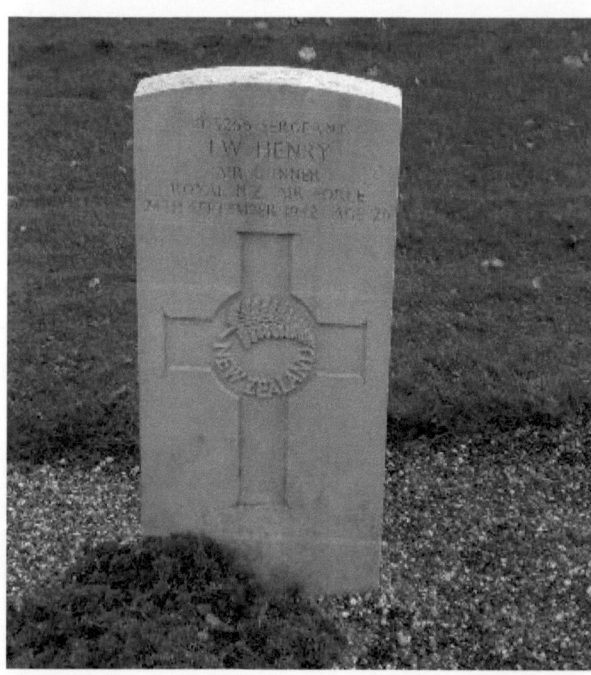

Sgt. (air gunner) John Wallace Henry, RNZAF (New Brighton, Canterbury, New Zealand)
Age 26.
Found near Skalo on October 19, 1942
Buried October 22, 1942.
Grave 4

A Halifax aircraft (bomber) from no.10 Squadron crashed October 1, 1942 in the sea at the southern Langeland.
The plane was on its way to bomb Flensburg.
All crew members perished. Five were buried in Odense and two at Svinø.

Sgt. (wireless operator/ air gunner)
Robert Francis Gourlay, RCAF (Canada)
Age 22.
Found near Vesteregn, Langeland on October 1, 1942
Buried October 7, 1942.
Grave 1
Inscription:
Blessed are the pure in heart for they shall see God

Sgt. (flight engineer) George William Spowart, RAF (Doncaster, Yorkshire, England)
Age 22.
Found near Vesteregn, Langeland on October 1, 1942
Buried October 9, 1942.
Grave 2
Inscription:
Treasured memories of our dear son and brother George – till we meet again

Two unknown Royal Air Force airmen, washed ashore near Nysted and Holeby, Lolland on September 26, 1942.
Buried in common grave on October 7, 1942. Grave 1b and 1c (at first buried together with Gourlay in grave 1 but later exhumed in order to be identified without any success and afterwards reburied in common grave)
Inscription:
Known unto God

A Halifax aircraft (bomber) from no.77 Squadron crashed on March 30, 1943 in the Baltic Sea.
The plane was on a bombing raid to Berlin. All crew members perished. One was buried at Svino. The rest of the crew is supposed to have disappeared in the sea.

Sgt. (flight engineer) James Middleton Donald, RAF (volunteer, Wishaw, Lanarkshire)
Age 26.
Found at Albuen near Nakskov on June 7, 1943
Buried June 10, 1943 as unknown – but with a cigarette case of silver with the initials J.M.D.
Identified after the war.
Grave 34
Inscription:
Ever remembered

90

A Stirling aircraft (bomber) from no. 7 Squadron crashed on April 21, 1943 near Kirke Stillinge, Western Zealand.

The aircraft participated in a bombing raid towards Stettin the night, when approximately 20 allied aircrafts crashed over Denmark. On its way back it was attacked three times by a German Messerschmitt and was at last so damaged that it crashed. One (Donald Smith see p. 59) survived and succeeded as the first allied airman to escape to Sweden. The other seven crew members were killed and were all buried at Svino.

Sgt. (air gunner) Dennis Charles Farley, RAF (volunteer, England.) Age unknown Buried April 24, 1943. Grave 6a

Warrant officer James Stanley Marshall, RCAF, (Canada.) Age not known Buried April 24, 1943. Grave 6b

Squadron Leader (2nd. pilot)
Wilfred Albert Blake, RAF, (Canada.) Age not known
Buried April 24, 1943.
Grave 7

Sgt. (air gunner) Jack Lees, RAF (Volunteer, Stacksteads, Lancashire)
Age 33.
Buried April 24, 1943.
Grave 8
Inscription:
Deep in our hearts his memory is kept, we who loved him never forget

*Flight Lieutenant, Pilot,
Charles Woodbine Parish, RAF
(Volunteer, England) (more
about Parish p.65)
Age 28.
Buried April 24, 1943.
Grave 9b*

*Pilot officer (navigator) Elmer
Robert Vance, RCAF (Bethune,
Saskatchewan, Canada)
Age 25.
Buried April 24, 1943.
Grave 9c*

Warrent Officer (wireless operator/air gunner)
Louis John Krulicki, RCAF (Kitchener, Ontario, Canada)
Age 22.
Buried April 24, 1943.
Grave 10
Inscription:
God gave you life, we love you. Now you have returned to him, who gave you life.

A Stirling aircraft (bomber) from no. 90 Squadron crashed on April 21, 1943 near Halskov, Korsoer.
The aircraft crashed on its way back from a bombing raid towards Rostock. All crew members were killed and were found in the sea along the coast between Korsoer and Reersoe.
Two crew members were buried at Bispebjerg Cemetery in Copenhagen.
Five crew members were buried at Svinoe.

Sgt. (navigator/bomber) Norman Shield, RAF (volunteer, England)
Age not known.
Found floating in The Great Belt on May 24, 1943
Buried May 26, 1943.
Grave 25

Sgt. (air gunner) John Desmond Lindrea, RAF (volunteer, Shalford, Surrey, England)
Age 25
Found floating in The Great Belt near Reersoe on May 27, 1943
Buried May 31, 1943.
Grave 28
Inscription:
O valiant heart

Sgt. (flight engineer) Cyril Leslie Cruttenden, RAF (volunteer, England)
Age not known.
Found floating in The Great Belt on May 28, 1943
Buried May 31, 1943.
Grave 30

*Pilot Officer Sydney Nelson Cross,
RNZAF (Tuapeka Mouth, Otago,
New Zealand)
Age 24
Found floating in The Great Belt
near Reersoe on May 27, 1943
Buried May 31, 1943.
Grave 31*

*Sgt. (air gunner) Edwin Marley
Offen, RAF
(Volunteer, England)
Age not known
Found at Lejodde, strech of coast at
the estate of Kruusesminde north of
Halskov on June 9, 1943
Buried June 12, 1943.
Grave 33*

A Halifax aircraft (bomber) from no. 158 Squadron crashed April 21, 1943 over The Great Belt near The Cliff of Droesselbjerg, Western Zealand
The aircraft was on its way home from a bombing raid towards Stettin. All members of the crew perished and were buried at Svinoe.

Sgt (air bomber) David Frank Rawlinson Banks, RAF (volunteer, Worting, Hampshire, England)
Age 20.
Buried April 24, 1943.
Grave 9a
Inscription: He lives forever in the hearts of those who love him. God bless. Beloved.

Sgt (air gunner) Michael Joseph Fitzgerald, RAF
(Volunteer, England)
Age unknown
Buried April 24, 1943.
Grave 11

*Sgt. (navigator) Henry Frederick
Daniel Lay, RAF (volunteer,
London, England)
Age 31
Buried April 24, 1943.
Grave 12
Inscription:
In loving memory of my darling
husband Harry. Always in my heart.
Your wife Peggy.*

*Sgt (wireless operator) George
William Cole, RAF (volunteer,
Twickenham, Middlesex, England)
Age 35
Buried April 24, 1943.
Grave13
Inscription:
A daily thought. An everlasting
memory.*

Flight Lieutenant, Pilot
David James Donaldson, RAF
(Whitby Yorkshire, England)
Age 34
Washed ashore near Droesselbjerg
and found on May 5, 1943
Buried May 7, 1943.
Grave 17
Inscription:
I spread my wings and keep my
promise.

Sgt (flight engineer) Leonard
Whyatt, RAF (Oldham, Lancashire,
England)
Age 23
Washed ashore near Droesselbjerg
and found on May13, 1943.
Buried May 14, 1943.
Grave.19
Inscription:
Winds of heaven blow gently here,
where lies sleeping one we love so
dear

Flight Lieutenant (navigator)
Wilfred John Parsons, RAF
(volunteer, Cowes, Isle of Wight)
Age 25
Washed ashore on the coast
between Droesselbjerg and Kirke
Stillinge on May 18, 1943
Buried May 21, 1943.
Grave.23
Inscription:
Sweet are the memories, silently
kept, of one we loved and will
never forget

Pilot officer George Harold Willis,
RAF (volunteer, Southern
Rhodesia)
Age 26
Washed ashore on the coast
between Droesselbjerg and Kirke
Stillinge on May 18, 1943
Buried May 21, 1943.
Grave 24
Inscription:
Rather Deathe than false of faythe

A Stirling aircraft (mine laying) from no. 75 Squadron crashed in the night between April 28 and 29, 1943 over The Baltic Sea/ Southern Great Belt
The aircraft had participated in mine laying in The Baltic Sea.
All members of the crew were killed but only two were found and buried at Svino.
The others must have disappeared in the ocean.

Sgt (air gunner) Harry Pears Holme, RAF
(Volunteer, Lower Ince, Lancashire,
England)
Age 35
Found near Nakskov on June 24,1943
Buried June 28, 1943.
Grave 37
Inscription:
Nobly he gave his life for us that we might
still live

Sgt (air gunner) Malcolm Edward John
Shogren, RNZAF, Auckland, New Zealand
Age 29
Found floating in Korsoer habour on June
2,1943
Buried June 5, 1943.
Grave 27

A Stirling aircraft (mine laying) from no. 75 Squadron crashed in the night between April 28 and 29, 1943 over The Baltic Sea southwest of Lolland
The aircraft was going to lay out mines in The Bay of Kiel. All crew members were killed in the crash and were buried at Svinoe.

Sgt (flight engineer) Clifford Abbott, RAF
(Volunteer, Clifton, York, England)
Age 21
Found near Kappel south of Nakskov on
April 29, 1943
Buried May 1, 1943.
Grave 16
Inscription:
Of such is the kingdom of God

Sgt (air gunner) John Thomas
Glendinning, RAF (volunteer, England)
Age unknown.
Washed ashore near Kappel south of
Nakskov on May 14, 1943
Buried May 18, 1943.
Grave 20

Wt. Officer (wireless operator/ air gunner) Ernest Roy Jenkins, RNZAF,
(Waharoa, Auckland, New Zealand)
Age 25.
Washed ashore near Kappel south of Nakskov on May 15, 1943.
Buried May 18, 1943.
Grave 21

Sgt (air gunner) George Phillips, RAF
(Volunteer, Ilford, Essex, England)
Age 28
Washed ashore near Kappel, south of Nakskov
on May 23, 1943
Buried May 26, 1943.
Grave26
Inscription:
So dearly loved, so greatly missed

Wt. Officer (navigator)
James Alexander Ramsay, RCAF
(Orillia, Ontario, Canada)
Age 26
Washed ashore near Kappel south
of Nakskov on May 11, 1943
Buried May 14, 1943.
Grave 18
Inscription:
"I will fear no evil; for Thou are
with me, thy rod and staff they
comfort me".
Psalm 23,4.

Pilot Officer Desmond Lewis
Thompson, RNZAF (Onehunga,
Auckland, New Zealand)
Age 21
Found near Kappel south of
Nakskov on April 29, 1943
Buried May 1, 1943.
Grave 15

Flight sergeant John Muir Williams,
RAAF
(East St. Kilda, Victoria, Australia)
Age 23
Found near Kappel, south of Nakskov on
April 29, 1943
Buried May 1, 1943.
Grave 14
Inscription:
John, beloved husband of Rose.

Grav nr. 22:

Body of unknown allied airman. Washed ashore near Korsoer and
found May 15, 1943. Buried May 18, at Svino Cemetery
Inscription:
Known unto God

Grav nr. 29:

Body of unknown allied airman. Found floating in The Great Belt
on May 28,1943.
Buried May 31, 1943 at Svino Cemetery
Inscription:
Known unto God

Grav nr. 32:

Body of unknown allied airman. Found near Nakskov on June 8,
1943
Buried June 12, 1943 at Svino Cemetery
Inscription:
Known unto God

A Lancaster aircraft from no. 619 Squadron crashed over The Baltic Sea on the night between February 15 and 16, 1944

The aircraft had been bombing Berlin and was hit by the Germans. All members of the crew were killed. Three were buried at Svino. The others seem to have disappeared in the ocean.

Flying Officer (air gunner) Phillip James Coleman, RAF (volunteer, England)
Age 21
Found near Errindlev, south of the road Rodby-Nysted, Lolland on June 3,1944
Buried June 6, with grave site ceremony June 18, 1944.
Grave 77
Inscription:
Awaiting the Kingdom

Flying Officer William Henry Charles Pateman, RAF (volunteer, England)
Age unknown
Found near Nakskov on April 22,1944
Buried April 30, with grave site ceremony May 5, 1944.
Grave 65

Flying officer, Pilot Robert Mons Rumble, RCAF
(Oak Ridges, Ontario, Canada)
Age 23
Found near Bandholm, Lolland on May 19, 1944
Buried May 22, with grave site ceremony May 28, 1944. Grave 72 (according to the church register) but 73 (according to CWGC)
Inscription:
I have fought a good fight, I have finished my course, I have kept the faith.

A Halifax aircraft from no. 77 Squadron crashed over Guldborgsund the night between April 23 and 24, 1944
The aircraft should lay out mines near Rostock but was hit by the Germans and caught fire over The Baltic Sea, whereupon it crashed in Guldborgsund. Four members of the crew survived and were helped to Sweden. Three were killed and buried at Svino.

Sgt (flight engineer) Glyn Jones, RAF
(Llanfairfechan, Caernarvonshire, Wales, England)
Age 32
Found near Nykoebing Falster on April 24, 1944.
Buried April 30, with grave site ceremony May 5, 1944
Grave 64
Inscription:
Eu henwau'n perarogli sydd, a'u hun. Mor dawel yw
(Uncertain: Their names are embalming as themselves. Is so quiet)

*Sgt (air gunner) William Henry
Loverock, RAF (volunteer, England)
Age unknown
Found near Bandholm, Lolland on
May 23, 1944
Buried May 26, 1944 with grave site
ceremony May 28, 1944
Grave 74*

*Flight sergeant Paul Derrick Sykes,
RAF (volunteer, England)
Age unknown
Found near Sakskobing, Lolland on
April 24, 1944
Buried April 30, with grave site
ceremony May 5, 1944
Grave 63
Inscription:
He gave his life for those he loved,
and those he loved remember.*

A Halifax aircraft from no. 102 Squadron crashed over Smaalands Ocean the night between April 23 and 24, 1944

The aircraft participated in a mine laying operation in The Baltic Sea and must have been hit by the Germans. All members of the crew were killed. Three disappeared in the ocean. One was buried at Omo. Three were buried at Svino.

Sgt (wireless operator/air gunner) Christopher George Woplin, RAF (Volunteer, Surrey, England) Age 21 (His father was also killed in the war) Found near Orenaes, Falster on May 11, 1944 Buried May 16, with grave site ceremony May 18, 1944. Grave 69 Inscription: A beautiful memory, a smiling face, a joving son, I can never replace. Mother

Pilot officer (air bomber) Ivan Arnold Weir, RCAF (Belmont, Manitoba, Canada) Age 22 Found near Karrebaekstorp, Zealand July 2, 1944. Buried as unknown July 3, with grave site ceremony July 9, 1944. Identified after the war. Grave 82 Inscription: God called him in out of the night. Remembered by mother, dad, Jean and Ruth.

*Flying Officer Alexander Henry Hall, RAF
(Volunteer, Malpas, Cheshire, England)
Age 27
Found by the Germans on October 4,
1944 near Airbase Avno and buried there
close to the coast. Exhumed on request of
the English authorities on February 6,
1946 and reburied February 10, 1946 at
Svino Memorial Grove.
Grave 92
Inscription:
No length of time can take away the
thoughts of you from day to day.*

**A Lancaster aircraft from no. 405 Squadron crashed near Allindemagle the
night between August 16 and 17, 1944**

The aircraft had participated in a bombing raid towards Stettin and was hit by the
Germans on its way home, whereupon it crashed. Six members of the crew survived
the crash, of which four managed to escape to Sweden, while two were captured by
the Germens. One was killed and buried at Svino.

*Pilot Officer (air gunner) Philip Arthur
Musgrave, RCAF (Canada)
Age unknown
Found at the crash site August 17, 1944
Buried August 17, with grave site
ceremony August 20, 1944.
Grave 84*

A Lancaster aircraft from no. 75 Squadron crashed at Oerslev Kohave, South Zealand the night before September 12, 1944

The aircraft had participated in a mine laying operation over The Baltic Sea, but was hit by the Germans and caught fire, whereupon it crashed. During the crash the aircraft hit a house, belonging to the Pommergaard family, and five members of the family were killed as well as five members of the crew. Two members of the crew were buried at Oerslev Cemetery, and three were buried at Svino Cemetery. Two members of the crew survived the crash, and one of them managed to escape to Sweden while the other one was captured by the Germans. (see more p.72)

Flight sergeant (air gunner) William James Victor Boyd, RNZAF (Mapua, Nelson, New Zealand)
Age 20
Found at the crash site on September 12, 1944
Buried September 12, with grave site ceremony September 17, 1944
Common grave 88

Flight sergeant (wireless operator/air gunner)
John Patrick Arthur Giles, RNZAF (Christchurch, New Zealand)
Age 21
Found at the crash site on September 12, 1944
Buried September 12, with grave site ceremony September 17, 1944
Common grave 88

Pilot Officer (navigator) John Bernard Gudgeon, RNZAF (Christchurch, New Zealand)
Age 23
Found at the crash site September 12, 1944
Buried September 12, with grave site ceremony September 17, 1944
Grave 88a

A Halifax aircraft from no.77 Squadron crashed over Smaaland Ocean the night before February 15, 1945

The aircraft had participated in a mine laying operation in The Baltic Sea and was hit by the Germans. All members of the crew were killed in the crash and were found at different places and buried at different cemeteries. Two were buried at Brarup Cemetery, Falster, one at Stubbekoebing Cemetery and one at Bogo. One was buried at Skelskoer Cemetery and two at Svino Cemetery.

Flying Officer James Ritchie, RAF (England)
Age 24 (born October 15,1920)
Washed ashore at Vesterhave beach near Karrebæk on May 7, 1945.
Buried May 11, 1945.
Grave 90

Sgt (air gunner) Ronald Edward Russell, RAF (volunteer, Tunbridge Wells, Kent, England)
Age 20
Found at the south coast of Knudshoved Spit near Vordingborg on June 10, 1945
Buried May 14, 1945
Grave 91
Inscription:
Sacred memories of our only son, whilst doing his duty God took him to rest.

A Lancaster aircraft from no. 44 Squadron crashed March 7, 1945 – presumably in The Baltic Sea.

The aircraft had participated in a bombing raid towards Sassnitz, Poland. The whole crew was killed in the crash but only one was found and buried. The others disappeared in the ocean.

Sgt (flight engineer) William Christopher Thornton, RAF (volunteer, Cashel, Tipperary, Irland)
Age 28
Found in Storstroemmen (steam of water) by a fisherman in June 1946.
Buried June 23, 1946
Grave 93
Inscription:
Sacred heart of Jesus, have mercy on his soul. R.I.P.

A Lancaster EE 138 from no. 460 Squadron crashed near Stadil, Western Jutland September 4, 1943

The aircraft had participated in a bombing raid towards Berlin and caught fire on its way back over Jutland. The aircraft exploded in the crash and at the crash site only a torso was found, which the Germans buried at the site.

I June 1947 the crash site was examined, but only the torso was found together with some material from an Australian battle uniform. Therefore the body was supposed to be one of the four (out of eight) airmen from Royal Australian Air Force. (See more p.26)

Squadron leader Carl Richard Kelaher, RAAF (London, England) Age 30
Warrant Officer Cyril Augustine Walsh, RAAF (Victoria, Australia) Age 30
Warrant Officer Ewin Garth Carthew, RAAF (South Australia) Age 21
Flying Officer Sydney Milton Forrester, RAAF (South Australia) Age 22
Found at the crash site and buried by the Germans September 4, 1943.
Exhumed and tried to be identified June 3, 1947.
Sent to Svino Cemetery and reburied June 13, 1943
Grave 97
Inscription:
Known unto God

Grave 66a and 66b:

Found near Kappel, close to Nakskov May 5, 1944
Buried May 8, 1944 with grave site ceremony May 14, 1944
Two unknown allied airmen buried in the same grave (no. 66). After the war tried to be identified and reburied in separate graves (no. 66a and 66 b)

Reflection:

Many years have passed since World War 2 took place.

Other wars have raged - wars that have also involved young people from the countries who during World War 2 represented the Allies, and in these years we are fighting against terrorism in many parts of the world.

One might therefore ask: why continue to remember those, who died so many years ago?

Former and now deceased church council chairman at Svino, Kurt Henriksen, always said, "When you have forgotten the graves from the recent war, you are only thinking of a new war. I hope, these graves will never be forgotten! "

I think, he had the quote from somewhere else, but I do not know from where it comes, and although the quote gives food for thoughts, it is probably not that simple anymore. Often some continue to remember the graves of the recent war, while others continue to think of new wars, new power demonstrations, new ways in which to get their own will, politics or religion carried through.

Can we find any help in religion here?

Or have we gone far beyond a religious understanding of life?

I write from a Christian understanding of life and would venture to say that it is exactly in hopelessness, the Christian faith can give us hope, in the midst of discouragement, it can bring us courage and in the middle of doubt that faith again can begin to sprout.

I fully understand and respect that many other people might have a different religious understanding of life and find faith, hope and strength there.

But it is when we are pressed and harassed and are having difficulty in finding a meaning in anything that we need to pray and powerless need to put our lives in the hands of God - not in order to leave our responsibility as humans there and be passive but in order to find strength to go on living the life that we have to, with all the challenges in this life.

It's actually the only thing that makes sense, when everything, we are living for, is suddenly snatched away from us.

It could be when an old person suddenly loses his life partner through an entire human life.

Or when a young couple has to say goodbye to an infant, who was never able to live.

Or when some New Zealanders are deeply touched standing in front of a grave on the other side of the Earth, because they remember how he, who lies in the grave, with his death so completely changed his mother's life - the mother who was the family's grandmother, and who never saw her own son's grave, and about whom it is told that she a few years later died of "a broken heart".

Or when an old man, who was the only survivor of a crashed aircraft in World War 2, visiting his comrades' graves and tells that he through all the years have been wondering why he himself was so fortunate to survive while the others perished.

Or ....well, each of us can think of plenty of violent and meaningless situations where the only thing bringing meaning into meaninglessness, is in prayer to put our lives in God's hand and trust that something greater than ourselves will carry us through here.

When, therefore, we continue together with hundreds of people year after year to commemorate the fallen airmen, when we gather at Svino on May 4th in the evening, it is because, we recognize ourselves and our loss in them and in their surviving fellow airmen, in their friends and in their families.

It makes sense to remember and remind ourselves and each other that in the midst of meaninglessness it may make sense to put our lives in the hands of God and pray "Thy will be done", because in this situation my own will is not enough - and then again try to be able to take up the challenges coming to us in a life that fortunately also provides us with lots of joy and love.

Explanations of words:

Liber Daticus	= A notebook belonging to the vicarage in which the vicar can write about special happenings in the parish or in the vicarage.
RAF	= Royal Air Force
RAAF	= Royal Australian Air Force
RNZAF	= Royal New Zealand Air Force
RCAF	= Royal Canadian Air Force
USAAF	= United States of America Air Force
P/O	= Pilot Officer
Lt/O	= Lieutenant Officer
Wt/O	= Warrant Officer
Fl/O	= Flight Officer
Sgt.	= Sergeant
W/O	= Wireless Operator
Sqdr.	= Squadron
DFC	= Distinguished Flying Cross
CWGC	= Commonwealth War Graves Commission

Source material:

The Church Register for the church district of Svino
The cemetery registers of Svino church district
The archive of Svino Memorial Grove
Kong-Svino website (koeng-svinoe-sogn.dk)
Anders Bjornvad: Fallen allied airmen 1939-1945
Helge William Gram: Shot down over Denmark 1940-45
Letters from Helge Gram
Roskilde Diocese Magazine June 1994 – 45. Volume – no. 6 – article of Mette Magnusson about Svino Memorial Grove
Palle Jensen: The book of Svino
N.M. Schaiffel-Nielsen: Airbase Avno (short version on the internet)
Anders Straarup: airmen.dk
Wikipedia and websites of several British and American squadrons as well as for specific aircrafts
Commonwealth War Graves Register over deceased persons of the two world wars.
Copies and notes from a friendly custodian/guardian Mr. Ferdinand M. Dessente of the American War Cemetery Ardennes, Neuville-en-Condrots, Belgium.
Register from Magraaten, American War Cemetery, Netherlands
Booklet received from Ejvind Friis Jensen in 1998 about the American airmen, who have been buried at Svino, and about the Memorial Stone on Arlington Cemetery, USA.
Jorgen Nielsen: First out of Denmark – about Donald Smith and his escape through Denmark to Sweden.
Booklet from 1943 written by the father of Pilot Officer Charles Woodbine Parish, received in a copy from Mr. Ron Wellings